ORANGE COUNTY WOMEN'S JAIL

A Journey Behind Bars With The Women of Sector 14

JENNIFER SWEET

Paddon Press ✿ Los Angeles

Copyright © 2011 by Jennifer Sweet

All rights reserved.

Published and printed in the United States of America

ISBN-10: 0615530206
ISBN-13: 978-0615530208 (Paddon Press)

No part of this book may be reproduced or transmitted in any form or by any means, electronic or mechanical, including photocopying, recording or by any information storage or retrieval system, without written permission from the author.

ABOUT THE AUTHOR

Jennifer Sweet was a blissfully ignorant 22-year-old recent college graduate living the good life in sunny Orange County, California; but misplaced trust in a deviant, drug-running boyfriend led her into a dark corner of the O.C. underworld known as Orange County Women's Jail. Jennifer took daily notes of her experiences during her two-year stay at OCWJ, and *Orange County Women's Jail* is a compilation of those notes. Some names, but not all, have been changed.

CONTENTS

	Introduction	1
1	Whitney and Cee-Cee	4
2	Cynthia, Lisa and Ardith	20
3	Myra	31
4	Parker's Pants, Tracy's Dog, Meghan's Tat and Edward's Religion	38
5	Antoinette's Mysterious Visitor and Maria's Dilemma	48
6	Debbie Does Dayroom and Cee-Cee's Secrets	55
7	LaTesha	62
8	Roof Rec	68
9	Linda and the Weed Whacker	72
10	Jail Lesbianism	84

ORANGE COUNTY WOMEN'S JAIL

11	Dana Allman	89
12	Goodbyes	97
	Epilogue	103

JENNIFER SWEET

Be thine own palace, or the world's thy jail.

~John Donne

INTRODUCTION

I was once a blissfully ignorant twenty-two-year-old recent college graduate living the good life in sunny Orange County, California; but misplaced trust in a deviant, drug-running boyfriend led me into a dark corner of the O.C. underworld known as Orange County Women's Jail. The "Housewives of Orange County" here include murders of husbands, maimers of mistresses and torturers of children. Two years of immersion in their presence while fighting my own case was like spending twenty years in an alternate universe. The experience was surreal, with ludicrous, ridiculous or tragic events occurring daily. Murderers, thieves, prostitutes, drug addicts and scam artists of every ilk were thrown together in this concrete-enclosed melting pot, and the results were always unexpected and endlessly fascinating.

There was the extraordinarily-troubled and intensely-insecure Ardith Cribbs, who shot her husband to death while he was handcuffed naked to their bed; the petite, savvy and wealthy Lisa Peng, who stabbed her husband's mistress to death and smothered their love child in a brutal attack; friendly but rageful prostitute Whitney Millano, whose mother sold her for drugs when she was two and whose father then decapitated her mother; and then there was Tracy Russell, arrested for bestiality after twice forcing sex upon her neighbor's male dog.

Many aspects of jail life were hellish, and the deprivation and isolation from family, friends, pets, loved-ones, nature and free will was overwhelming. It was a place of deep misery, night terrors and intense grief. But amid the darkness was a lot of light; and alongside the pain and suffering was humor, ridiculousness and outright absurdity. The experience that I thought would crush me instead enlightened me and expanded my awareness and understanding of life and my fellow human travelers. More than anything, I witnessed the resilience of the human spirit, and learned that even in the deepest, darkest places of the most deviant soul, there is much good to be found. Love, humor, compassion and wishes for goodness and peace are not exclusive to the more financially-blessed and respected denizens of Orange County; they also exist in the many miscreants the community keeps locked away in cold concrete rooms behind high walls in the City of Santa Ana. This is their story.

JENNIFER SWEET

I was kind of excited about going to jail the first time, and I learned some great dialogue.

~Quentin Tarantino

anything ever portrayed on those programs or others about life in Orange County.

On this, my first morning on the inside, consciousness crept back over me and the solace of sleep faded away as the booming voice of an unknown woman pierced my awareness and demanded my full attention. She was thirty-something, about 5'7" and 130 pounds with beautiful, shiny, straight brown hair that reached the middle of her back. Her heavy black eyeliner and mascara enhanced her rough-but-strikingly-attractive features, but the tattoos running up and down her arms and neck detracted from her beauty. The naked woman covering her left forearm was the first to catch my eye, but the others were equally evocative and bold. She was smiling from ear-to-ear for no apparent reason. I quickly realized that she was trying to coax me out from under my scratchy jail-issue blanket and out of my cell. Only then did I notice that my door had been electronically popped-open by the deputies responsible for monitoring us.

"Come on, get your ass out here before I come in and drag it out. Don't think I won't."

Standing before my cell door in her oversized jail-issue blue jumpsuit with a hand on her hip, I immediately got the sense that she was coming as friend, not foe.

"What's going on," I asked, unsure of the protocol.

"We get out of our rooms twice a day for two hours at a time. We just hang out in the dayroom, play cards, watch TV. You know, just hang out. Come on, get outta that hole."

"Sure, okay," I said, buttoning up my own rumpled jumpsuit and running a hand through my bed hair.

I was in Sector 14. There were several two-level sectors that formed a circle around a large tinted glass dome that housed the deputies who sat and watched us day and night. They spoke to us and gave demands via speakers on the walls of our cells and walked through each sector periodically to check up on our activities. Each sector housed a different band color. White-band sectors had first-timers and inmates who weren't considered hostile or threatening to one another. Yellow-banders had longer rap sheets and had gotten in a fight or two while incarcerated. Lesbians were also categorized as yellow-banders, since the deputies watched them closely for any signs of unauthorized intimate behavior. Then there were the orange-banders who were considered chronic fighters and who simply couldn't get along with anyone. Red-banders were the most violent of all. Women with red bands had at some point during their stay assaulted a deputy or deputies. The amount of respect one received was based upon the color of one's band. White-banders deferred to yellow-banders, yellow to orange, and orange to red. But at the bottom of the hierarchy were the loathsome blue-banders. A blue band signified one of three things: 1) The person was a snitch, 2) the person was a child molester/killer or 3) The person's crime was so heinous that if they were put in the general population they would be beaten or killed. A blue band meant PC – protective custody. They were never allowed around anyone else without a deputy present. They were hated, spit upon in court, and generally the recipients of all the other inmates' pent-up rage and hostility.

Although I was a white-bander, I and other first-time white-banders were housed in the blue-bander sector because of overcrowding. There wasn't enough room in the white-band sector, so a number of us took up residence in the PC's neighborhood. They had different dayroom times than us, picked up their meal trays separately, and had visitors separately. We could talk with them any time we wished through the cell doors, which were mostly composed of steel and bullet-proof glass, as well as through our vents. We just were never allowed to be physically near them.

Stepping out into the open space of our dayroom with this bright-eyed, beautiful-but-hard-looking woman grinning at me gave me the eerie feeling that all was not well. I looked around and saw approximately 15 other women of all persuasions and orientations emerging from their individual cells. They all walked to their usual

1
WHITNEY AND CEE-CEE

It was just another flawlessly beautiful June morning in sun-soaked Orange County, the conservative, Republican-ruled span of land that lies south of Los Angeles. Just another day for the majority of law-abiding, upstanding citizens who reside in this vast suburb of manicured lawns and mini-mansions. But not just another day for me. I had been pulled from Southern California dreamin' into the confines of a Southern California nightmare. Never arrested before, I found myself waking up in jail days after graduating from college and just a week after turning 22 on drug trafficking charges. Unbeknownst to me, my boyfriend was transporting massive quantities of cocaine...in my car...while I was with him. The nightmare that I was sure would be cleared up within a week ultimately took two years to resolve. All the while, I witnessed the other side of Orange County – the side never revealed on such programs as "Housewives of Orange County" or "The Hills." The underbelly of the OC was far more fascinating, intriguing, mysterious and entertaining than corners and tables and interacted with one another as though their movements had been carefully choreographed. There was a fluidity and uniformity of motion that connected each of these unusual, miscreant creatures like an invisible string.

"Snap out of it, kid," Whitney barked. "Come over here and talk to me. You look lost."

I walked with her and sat at one of eight round stainless steel tables bolted to the floor throughout the room. The TV, attached high on the wall out of our reach, was blaring the news, but no one seemed to notice.

"I'm sorry, but I just don't know anything about jail," I explained. "It's all kind of confusing."

"Oh, fuck that shit, girl. Jail ain't no thing. Once ya' learn the rules and how to break 'em, you'll be just fine. What's your name?"

"Jennifer. Jennifer Sweet."

"Is that right? Well, I'm Whitney. Whitney Millano. Ha-ha! Why are you so damn formal, Jen? Lighten' up, babe, or you'll never make it in here," she added. "Hey Cee-Cee, get your ho ass over here and meet Jennifer. Jennifer Sweet. This girl's a trip."

The Black woman's voice I had heard earlier in the morning reprimanding Whitney through the vents came sashaying toward us in the body of a 26-year-old Caucasian, petulantly-pouting prostitute with medium length curly light brown hair. "Whas up?" she asked, her hand resting on her hip and her large dark eyes penetrating my skull. When Cee-Cee looked at you, you really knew you were being looked at.

"This is my new friend, Cee. She's alright, but she's a little spun. Another virgin."

"She looks like she belongs on a college campus, not in this shit hole," Cee-Cee spat. "So you never been to jail? How ya likin' it so far?" she asked, while taking a seat opposite me.

"Well," I replied, a bit reluctantly. "To be honest, I hate it. No offense, but there are a lot of weirdoes around here." This aroused some hearty laughter from each of them.

"This is a fuckin' loony bin, that's for damn sure, but it's not a bad loony bin. Really, it's not," Whitney said, piquing my curiosity. Noticing the look of disbelief on my face, she continued: "Don't worry about it, Cee and I will be your welcome wagon. Hang with us. We'll show your little good-girl ass the ropes. We won't fuck with ya. We're just a couple of hos doin' our part to make the county jail a better place. Ain't that right?" she asked Cee-Cee.

"Couldn't be no righter thang. We set ya' up. You look innocent as a baby's butt. Fuckers try ta' take advantage 'cause of that. Fuck those motha-fuckers. Shit, bitch… you got a runner?"

"A runner? As in a drug runner? No."

"Oh fuck, no – a runner. Someone who puts money on your books and is down for ya. You know, for commissary and shit," Cee-Cee continued.

"Commissary. What's that?" I inquired, baffled by this exchange.

"Damn, Whitney, you was right. This bitch is the fuckin' queen of virgins. Commissary comes every Tuesday and Friday. We order hygiene and candy and chips and shit, all kinds of stuff. Ya gotta have a runner to bring money so ya can set yourself up and all. My runner's my old man. Whitney's runner's her big bro. Who's your runner?" Cee asked once more.

"I guess that would be my Mom," I said, still trying to grasp what I had just been told. "You mean we get to 'shop' here?"

"Hell yeah!" screeched Whitney. "I sure as fuck couldn't survive too long in this place without my coffee and sugar fix. Those dumb-ass deputies know if they don't let us have our goodies they'll have a damn riot on their hands."

I sat and spoke at length with my first jail acquaintances for the rest of our dayroom time. They informed me of the rules and regulations, as well as how to get around them. They pointed out various women and told me what they were in for. They told me their stories, and I told them mine. My initial meeting with Whitney and Cee-Cee was an introduction into jail life that formed the basis of my eventual assimilation. But my actual time with them was to be both fleeting and intermittent. The turn-over rate in jail is considerably high and I saw a number of my new friends come and go (and very often come again) with great frequency. The stories Whitney and Cee-Cee shared with me that day were both touching and frightening.

Whitney was born in, as she put it, "sunny Southern California," the daughter of a prostitute mother and drug dealer father. Her parents were transients who lived each day in search of their next heroin fix. Mr. Millano had at least 11 other children by several different women before Whitney was born. When she was two years old and her father was away for an extended period of time, Whitney was sold by her mother to a heroin dealer in exchange for an insubstantial amount of the drug. When her father arrived back on the scene a couple weeks later and discovered what had transpired, he attacked his wife in a rage and decapitated her with a carving knife. He was consequently locked away in prison while Whitney was sent to an Orange County orphanage called Orangewood. As time went by, I would discover that a great number of my fellow inmates had resided at that institution at some point in their lives. Whitney lived there until her release at age 18. Along the way, she was periodically turned over to foster homes, in many of which she was molested, beaten and sometimes brutally raped. She grew into an angry young adult full of rage and self-hatred. She turned to drugs to ease her inner turmoil, turned to prostitution to support her habit, and turned to her "sisters and brothers" on the streets for family.

Despite Whitney's obvious and severe emotional trauma, and dire prospects for the future, she was upbeat, bright and charming. As long as you didn't make her angry, she was a loving and fun person. However, the seemingly most insignificant thing, such as a perceived put-down from a deputy, could trigger her underlying rage. And when it did, she would verbally release her fury on any and all around her. The deputies always handled force with force, and frequently resorted to pepper spray to subdue and overpower Whitney on these occasions. It always pained me to see her struggling and fighting with them, and writhing in pain from the spray. Her rage was a consequence of early, prolonged abuse; and its own consequence was even further abuse. It was tragic to witness. I realized then how futile it was to punish rather than rehabilitate Whitney, and all the others like her. And I knew that, since our correctional system was unlikely to change anytime soon, her future would most likely be just as dark as her past.

Whitney would one day be yellow-banded, and eventually red-banded for fighting with the deputies. But for now she was one of us, and we enjoyed her humor, private kindness, resilience and passion. She often entertained us with stories about her various tricks and their unique perversions. There was the man who took her into a motel room and smoked some rock cocaine before getting down to business. He stripped off all his clothes to reveal women's lingerie underneath. He had the hose, garters, brassiere, lacy panties, the works. Then he slipped on Whitney's high heels to walk around the room. She said, "Hey man, those are mine. It'll cost ya an extra $20 to wear those." He agreed to the extra cost and continued to walk seductively back and forth across the floor, his crotch barely contained in the panties and a mass of kinky hair pouring out of the bra. As Whitney watched in amusement and made whistling and cat-call sounds, the trick picked up a blue rubber racquet ball. A small slit had been cut into it, and he shoved it snugly onto his now erect penis. The man walked over to where Whitney was sitting on the bed and begged and pleaded with her to hit the ball as hard as she could. She said, "I can't do that, it'll hurt." He then proceeded to beg and plead with her even further, and finally offered to throw in an extra $50 for the service. This was enough motivation for Whitney, so she obliged. The man screamed out, "Harder, harder," and eventually got what he had come for. Whitney took the money and ran.

Another trick simply wanted nothing more than for her to get her feet filthy dirty and massage them all over a basketball while he masturbated. Her trouble was worth $100. Most of her stories were tinged with humor and sarcasm. Some, however, were wrought with pain. She was raped more than once, severely beaten more than once, and stabbed more than once. But it was her life and the only one she knew. Whitney would continue for the rest of her life to use her body to get the medicine to soothe her pain.

Although Whitney was my first mentor at OCWJ, Cee-Cee became my longest and closest friend. She showed me the proverbial ropes and taught me a thing or two extra on the side. She showed me how to make my jail-issue flat slippers more comfortable by sticking extra-absorbent feminine napkins inside each shoe. She told me to save my orange peels from breakfast each morning, let them dry out, and then bring them to her. When I did, she showed me how to get high "on a welfare motha's budget." She dug out the center of a feminine napkin and shoved the dried peels inside. She twisted some toilet paper into a long, thin ball and dipped the end in baby oil (available through commissary). Then she stuck the part with the baby oil into an electrical outlet and, to my surprise, it ignited. She lit the end of the pad and took a hit. "Ummmm... smooth." Cee offered me some of the goods, but I declined, citing my strict adherence to a healthy lifestyle. Her only response was a dry, "Nerd," and another long drag on the feminine napkin. Of course, "Nerd" was a term of endearment, especially considering the myriad other derogatory terms she had tucked away in her vocabulary.

Cee-Cee's story was a bit less violent, but much more adventurous than Whitney's. She was a prostitute, but was in on counterfeiting charges this time around. Her and her "homeboy," Ted, were making counterfeit money with a group of their close friends and raking in a bundle. They took the cash to Las Vegas and threw hundreds on a black jack or craps table in exchange for chips. They would play for a bit and then find a reason why they needed to move along; then they would cash their chips in for legitimate money. The crew spent weeks hitting different tables and different casinos. Everything was looking up and life was grand until she and Ted made the fateful decision to go to Disneyland. Cee and Ted were driving along the 5 freeway in Orange County when Ted got the uncontrollable urge to smoke some rock cocaine. As they neared the exit to Disneyland, Ted announced that he wanted to stop and smoke there. He said he had a year's pass, so he could get in and park amongst the mass of cars without having to worry about being seen by any cops. Cee-Cee said, "Hell no, I don't wanna go to any fuckin' Disneyland. This is bullshit!"

Ted replied, "Baby, come on. Please. I gotta get a hit or I'm gonna lose it. I need this baby, I really need this."

They pulled in and found what appeared to be a fairly secluded area. Just as he was holding the pipe up to take a hit, one of the park cops who patrol the parking lots in golf-carts cruised by and spotted him. Eye contact was established and the cop began driving in their direction. Ted flipped out while Cee-Cee screamed at him to "Get us the fuck outta here!" He started the car and spun out. He became confused and disoriented in the parking lot maze and couldn't remember which way the exit was. Around this time, he noticed about seven or eight other golf-cart cops chasing him and racing in and out of various aisles. The first guy had called for back-up, and it didn't help matters that Ted and Cee were in a brand new, bright orange Mustang. They sped in and out and all around the aisles of the Disneyland parking lot with golf-cart-cops in hot pursuit and pedestrians fleeing for cover until, at last, they were cornered and forced to surrender.

Not only were the drugs and paraphernalia confiscated, but the fake money and some of the manufacturing materials were also discovered. Cee-Cee was subsequently thrown in the Orange County Women's Jail, and Ted in the OC Men's Jail.

Cee-Cee begged and pleaded with a friend of hers to bail her out. He was very hesitant and needed assurance that she wouldn't skip out of town and leave him high and dry. She swore up and down that she would make all of her court appearances and that he would definitely get his money back. He eventually accepted her word and put up the cash. She never had any intentions of reporting to court and made plans to never see this man again. Unfortunately, a mutual friend told him what street she was working and he subsequently tracked her down. When he found her, he beat the living daylights out of her and bashed in the back of her head with the butt of his gun. As a result of this injury, she had seizures occasionally and had to take multiple medications for the problem.

When Cee-Cee sought medical treatment for her injuries, she was found out as a wanted person. She was returned to jail to face her charges. This time she was being held without bail. After a couple of days, she contacted another friend of hers who was an expert in forgery and had him make a false death certificate for her sister, even though she has no sister. She feigned profound grief and provided the certificate for the judge at her next court appearance. He was so touched by her sorrow and fooled by the forgery that he granted her two days in which to attend the funeral. Of course, she didn't return after those two days, as she had been ordered. She was free for about a month before an acquaintance got arrested and told the authorities of her whereabouts to get a break on his own charges.

When I asked Cee-Cee if Ted was her boyfriend, she chortled, "This ain't no boyfriend-girlfriend thang. This is a pimp-ho thang!" and then laughed that characteristic hearty guffaw that was immediately recognizable as Cee-Cee's. This woman was definitely in a class all her own.

If you want to know who your friends are,

get yourself a jail sentence.

~Charles Bukowski

2
CYNTHIA, LISA AND ARDITH

Being in the blue-bander sector, I met and became acquainted with a number of women who were in for high-profile cases. The individuals I have in mind had committed the most violent crimes of us all. Amazingly, though, they were some of the most considerate, gentle, "nice" people among us. There was Cynthia Medina who was on trial for torturing her ten-year-old nephew. A heavyset Mexican woman in her 30's with a spring in her step and an easy smile, Cynthia was eventually convicted of anally penetrating the boy so severely with a souvenir toy baseball bat that he was temporarily fitted with a colostomy bag. The torture was inflicted because the boy had played with marijuana cigarettes Cynthia had in an ashtray. She also burned his tongue with hot knives, whipped him with an electrical cord, bashed his face onto a sink, knocking out several teeth, as well as kicking him in the groin when he failed to do his chores. In the end, she was found guilty of these horrific deeds, but throughout her stay in jail, she was simply angelic. Everyone in the blue-bander sector became friends with

Cynthia Medina. She had a separate dayroom time than everyone else because of the nature of her case, but she managed to draw us all to her, nevertheless. She had a beautiful voice and loved to sing, so she would have the deputies turn our dayroom TV off so she could sing to us. When she asked for requests, a chorus of voices emanated from the cells with song ideas. We never tired of that shockingly-sweet voice. We weren't allowed a radio in jail and you miss music terribly when you're deprived of it for any length of time, so Cynthia was rather precious to us...despite her horrific history.

Cynthia also always shared her commissary with anyone who was in need. A candy bar here, coffee there. Anyone who asked was sure to receive from Cynthia. If a person didn't know any better, they would think she was one of the most genuinely caring, thoughtful people to grace the earth.

Although a harsh word never escaped her lips and she was as generous as one could be in such an environment, her crime clung to her everywhere she went. The people she sang for expressed their disdain for her behind her back. The people with whom she shared her commissary rejoiced at the news that she had been convicted. It's not that loyalties shifted. It's that loyalties never existed – only pseudo-loyalties, when needed or necessary.

Lisa Peng was another story. She was a wealthy, pretty, petite, Chinese businesswoman who spoke in broken English, was easy-going, and had an exceedingly gentle disposition. In contrast to Cynthia, Lisa was genuinely liked by us all. She was sweet, cute and funny, and although she was 44, she appeared much younger. Lisa was charged with stabbing to death her husband's mistress and smothering the baby boy the woman had conceived with him. In spite of the boundless rage and physical aggression that must have been required to commit such an act, Lisa came off as tiny, weak and passive. She was obsessed with staying pencil thin and spent every dayroom walking around and around the perimeter of the large space. It was unsettling to sit and watch this tiny little woman walk while trying to imagine her committing the crime for which she had been accused. It was the first time in my life that I had truly grasped the saying, "looks can be deceiving."

And then there was Ardith Cribbs. Ardith was a white-bander, like myself. At thirty-eight-years-old, she was thin with graying brown hair. She appeared to be from an upper-middle class background, and generally gave the appearance of refinement and style. Her crime: murdering her husband while he was naked and handcuffed to their bed posts. They had been engaging in some kinky sex acts when Gordon said something cruel and degrading that seriously set her off. She was never able to recall the exact words that propelled her into fury; all she knew is that they filled her with blind rage. She screamed and yelled at him while running to another room in the house. She heard him laughing, which infuriated her all the more. She emerged from the other room with a .357 Magnum, marched back to the bedroom, stood before Gordon at the foot of their bed and pulled the trigger four times. The naked man in handcuffs received all four bullets and died from one that lodged in his brain. Ardith then went to yet another room, reloaded the gun and returned it to its usual place.

She then phoned a cop friend of hers, with whom she had been having an affair, and rambled on and on about how she should have married him and how she had made numerous mistakes in her life. She hung up abruptly and wandered about the house. An hour later, she called the cop friend back, saying she had done something bad and was going to kill herself. Then she hung up on him again. The man called the local police and alerted them to her state of mind. The rest, as they say, is history.

Ardith gave the outward appearance of being the picture of normality, but as we all know, one can't judge a book by its cover. She said Gordon never abused her. He was a good provider, hard worker and a funny, intelligent man. From time to time when they were having sex he would become verbally sadistic and degrading. It was his personal perversion – a fetish of sorts. However, Ardith had no such inclinations and was deeply offended and perturbed by his games. Perturbed enough in the end to take his life.

Ardith had some problems that no doubt contributed to this seemingly blatant overreaction to Gordon's taunts. For one thing, she had worked in a bordello in Las Vegas for several years before meeting her husband. A place where she encountered a number of disturbing characters. She, like the prostitutes previously mentioned, dealt with men with off-beat desires and fantasies. Some wanted her to walk on them in spiked heels. Another wanted needles to be jabbed through his penis. Still others desired only to play dress-up and be berated. There was also the guy who liked to play "School," with Ardith as the teacher and himself as the bad student. He would pinch her butt or grab her breasts while she was in the middle of a lesson and she would punish him by saying, "Bad boy. Very bad boy," and slapping his penis swiftly with a ruler. Then there was Kyle. Kyle was supposedly the one who inflicted the most severe psychological trauma upon Ardith. He was a regular at the bordello who quickly became taken with her. He was a wealthy, charming, violent, sadistic, charismatic, enigma of a man, to hear Ardith tell it. He was an ugly person, yet every face in the room lit up when he made an entrance. People were inexplicably drawn to him and deferred to his every whim. According to Ardith, Kyle was a diamond broker involved in the international market of drugs for jewels. He was an extremely powerful man who frequently had his underlings break the legs of those who crossed him. Those who tried to take advantage of him, or otherwise severely ticked him off, mysteriously disappeared, never to be heard from again. Ardith made the connection in her mind between him and several women who had turned up missing from the bordello; women who had been considering leaving with inside knowledge of their tricks' illegal activities still in their heads.

Ardith quickly concluded that she could probably never escape the bordello with her life. She saw Kyle's charms recede when he began violently raping her on a daily basis. She said he had an unusually large penis that badly tore her on those occasions. During this period, when they were making love consensually he would rant on and on in graphic detail about dissecting her body and having sex with every mutilated part. Although disgusted and horrified by his sadistic comments and behavior, Ardith was too fearful to leave. She knew he would never let her go – she was his possession now. Kyle became increasingly paranoid about Ardith trying to run away, and as his insecurities grew so did the terrifying threats and perverse mind games that he used to keep her in a perpetual state of fear. She said he drugged her one evening and videotaped himself raping her limp body. He entered every orifice with extreme force and poured a small container of acid onto her right hip. It quickly ate the flesh away to the bone. When she awoke from her drugged state, she was oblivious to what had transpired, but felt the residual burning of the acid, and blood clotting around her aching rectum. Kyle showed her the video evidence of what had happened and told her that she was his property and he could do anything he wanted to her. He warned her never to even consider leaving, and said he would destroy her and her entire family if she ever tried.

Ardith shared an experience with me that demonstrated the lengths to which this man went in his efforts to maintain full control of her. The incident sounded surreal, and still strikes me as very difficult to believe. However, she insisted emphatically that it did in fact happen. It began as a simple drive around town. Kyle pulled the Mercedes next to an abandoned warehouse and instructed Ardith to get out and follow him. Once inside, they came face-to-face with five other people. Two were Kyle's bodyguards, one was Ardith's father, one was her mother, and the other was her younger sister. Kyle said, "What are you standing there for? Go say hi to your family."

Ardith stood frozen, looking on in awe. Her family lived in Oregon and never would have spontaneously visited her in Las Vegas. They knew she worked in a bordello, but they did not approve, nor did they know about Kyle. She took a few steps forward and said, "Mom?" then touched her mother's face. It was thick with make-up. Kyle released a wicked laugh. The family and bodyguards joined in the laughter while Ardith recoiled in horror at the sudden realization that the people before her were complete strangers. The faces, the bodies, the mannerisms were all those of her loved ones, but loved ones they definitely were not. Kyle explained that many of the people who turned up missing as a result of bad business with him were often given the option of avoiding death by agreeing to undergo extensive plastic surgery and taking part in the darker side of his underworld. He told her that the individuals would be assigned to observe the manner of a particular person and learn to precisely mimic them in every way. Surgery would then be performed to transform the man or woman into an exact physical and facial replica of the subject. Once this was completed, Kyle would have the real people killed, such as Ardith's family members, and replace them with these clones. He warned Ardith that that's what he would do to her if she ever left him or told anyone about his illegal undertakings. He told her that she would know her loved ones were dead, but that if she told anyone about the clones overtaking the roles of her parents and sister, they would simply think her insane and ignore her cries for help. She therefore never disclosed this information to her attorney, or revealed it during her trial. Although the prosecution made certain to impress upon the jury the significant degree to which Ardith's employment at the bordello reflected upon her character, no mention was ever made of the perverse horrors she experienced there or their ultimate impact upon her.

Eventually, Ardith escaped from the bordello and Kyle and returned to her family in Oregon. She left Kyle behind physically, but never psychologically. She was forever looking over her shoulder, and swore up and down that she saw the cloned family members from the warehouse on numerous occasions around her rural Oregon town. She said a limo followed her everywhere and stayed parked at the end of her street when she was home. In addition, she believed Kyle had somehow placed an implant in her brain before she left him because she was certain that other people were reading her thoughts. She endlessly complained to me about how much this particular problem disturbed her, saying once, out of the total blue, "It really pisses me off with this implant that I can't even have a God damn thought to myself."

Ardith's mental instability was severe and she was never able to rid herself of the profound fear and terror instilled in her by Kyle. Her most salient personality feature was paranoia. In her mind, everyone was potentially one of Kyle's "people." She even verbally assaulted me on a couple of occasions, accusing me of stealing her thoughts to use them against her in her trial. She also created an elaborate theory about what really happened that fateful night. She believed Gordon wasn't really killed, despite the fact that her family and friends saw his dead body at the funeral. She thought it was all a conspiracy concocted by Kyle and Gordon in conjunction with her cop friend (with whom she had been having an affair) and his fellow officers to destroy her and get her ultimately sentenced to death. No matter how often I pointed out the fact that she was not facing the death penalty, she clung to this theory.

Ardith Cribbs wasn't all conspiracy theories and horror stories, however. She was an average, although somewhat annoying, person the majority of the time. We often sat and played cards or chess while in the dayroom. We both participated in the usual women's jail activities such as gathering around and drooling over pictures of "real" food and desserts in magazines, and observing the complete silence rule when the Sector's favorites came on the television: The Andy Griffith Show and Soul Train. Ardith could be a kidder when she wanted to. She would occasionally tap me on the shoulder at mealtime and open her mouth wide to reveal a mushy mass of chewed-up jail food. Then she would emit the high-pitched titter that was her trademark laugh, and wrinkle her nose up as I told her how immature she was. Another one of Ardith's less desirable habits had to do with her facility with flatulence. I have never in my life heard anyone, male or female, fart so loudly or so frequently. These were earthquake-inducing emissions. And not the kind you want to be stuck in a 6' x 8' cell with.

Her personal habits, quite honestly, disgusted me. She seemed to have no respect whatsoever for the sensibilities of others. She would casually relate to me her latest discovery that her vagina was producing an unusual odor and would then take offense if I was so rude as to not respond. She pouted and whined constantly and always spoke in timid, little girl tones. In addition, she was by far the most insecure person I had ever met in my life. Not a day went by when she didn't ask me at least five times if I thought she was pretty or if I liked her or if I thought she was getting fat. Sometimes she would ask me, then she'd fart and I would be so disgusted by her that I couldn't even answer, so she would start pouting. To put it more simply, the woman drove me crazy. I felt very, very sorry for poor Gordon.

ORANGE COUNTY WOMEN'S JAIL

What was really horrifying about jail is that it really isn't horrifying. You adjust very easily.

~Roberta Victor

3
MYRA

One afternoon while I was playing gin rummy with Ardith and the rest of the girls were flitting around the dayroom with "All My Children" ringing out from the TV, we got a new girl. She walked through our sector door holding a bedroll tightly in her skinny, heavily scarred and bruised arms. She was about 5'9" and 115 pounds. She looked drawn and ill and was obviously coming down off of some heavy drugs. Cee-Cee promptly waltzed over to her and said, "Girl, you be tore up from the floor up. You must be kickin' some hard shit."

The girl looked up and said, "Hey Cee, what's up?"

"Myra, you look like shit warmed over! Put that crap away and come talk to me, homegirl."

Myra was a big-time heroin addict. The bruises and scars covering her body were a result of slamming –

jabbing the hypodermic needle into her flesh in search of functioning veins in which to release the heroin. She and Cee-Cee turned out to be friends from Beach Boulevard, the street they both worked, also known as "the ho stroll." She was brought in on solicitation and drug charges after she propositioned an undercover officer for sex. He flashed his badge and arrested her, but not until after he instructed her to stroke his penis a few times. She was "working" to get money for her drug of choice when she got busted. So severe was her habit that she continued to slam even after all of her surface veins had collapsed. She resorted to shooting up in her hands and fingers, then her feet. When it got to its worst point, she shot up in her eyelids, and, finally, in her tongue. She had to have that high. She felt she couldn't live without it. Abscesses were scattered haphazardly on her skin where her slamming had resulted in infections that grew until they oozed blood and pus. One in particular seemed to constantly leak blood from her left forearm. Myra had managed to smuggle some cocaine in. She always had a little plastic baggie of it lodged in her vagina in the (likely) event that she should get arrested. This particular trip to OCWJ was number 14 for her. She shared a bit of her stash with Cee-Cee and they both acted like hyperactive children for a few days, but that was the extent of the drugs-in-jail adventure.

A couple months later, while I was sitting at a table with a group of girls who were exchanging their drug connections' beeper numbers, I overheard Myra talking to Cee-Cee about Myra's upcoming trial. She said her 65-year-old pimp/"old man" had gone to Target and stolen a nice "respectable" dress for her to wear to court. She was now concerned about what she would do for shoes.

Cee-Cee suggested she tell him to go back and steal some that matched the dress. Myra thought this was a splendid idea and trotted over to the phone to call the gentleman.

Late that night, the deputies escorted in a somewhat unruly girl who didn't appear to be totally cognizant of her situation. They tried to get her to go into her cell, but she threw a fit and refused. As she was screaming at the top of her lungs, Myra appeared at her door, which was the one immediately to the left of the new girl's. As soon as the new girl saw this tall, thin apparition with long, flowing hair, she dropped to her knees and began to pray. "Oh my God!" she cried. "It's Jesus! Jesus, my savior, has come. Praise the Lord, praise the Lord! Save me, Jesus, from these deputy demons!" Myra scoffed and plopped back down on her bed. At this point, the girl threw a tantrum and raged on and on about the crucifixion of Christ and how her persecutors were going to burn in hell for their sins. Finally, the deputies called Myra back to her door and instructed her to tell the girl that Jesus wants her to go into the cell. Myra reluctantly complied. Her mere appearance brought the troubled woman to a state of worship once again. "Hey stupid," Myra snarled, "Get your ass in that cell and shut the fuck up." Amazingly enough, the girl bowed her head in reverence of the mighty one and crawled into the cell singing, "I once was lost, but now am found…" All night we were subjected to the repeated excruciating rendering of that song, with intermittent warnings from Jesus to "Shut the fuck up or I'm gonna rip your fuckin' head off!" The girl went to court early the following morning and never returned to our sector.

Many of the regulars to OCWJ were much like Myra. When things got too intense on the outside, or the drugs and food weren't coming in with sufficient regularity, they came to jail for a little rest, relaxation and recuperation. They were ensured three square meals a day, a warm place to sleep, protection from the elements and an opportunity to catch up with old friends. At times it seemed as though everybody knew everybody else – like one big extended family. They all lived together on the streets and vacationed together in jail. Aside from the occasional murderess or child abuser, the vast majority of the inmates were in on drug, petty theft or prostitution charges. These women weren't violent people; they were desperate but resilient people. The aggressive, combative women portrayed so vividly in television and movie versions of jail life were few and far-between in real life. Physical confrontations did occur, but they were rare. Very common, though, were verbal attacks that generally ended with an eventual slow fizzling-out of tension, and a disintegration of conflict. The end of one such exchange went as follows:

LaTesha: You fuckin' ugly-assed bitch. You ain't nothin' but a $10 ho!

Cee-Cee: Hey mutha-fucker! What you got against hos?!

LaTesha: I ain't got nothin' against no hos. Just *cheap* hos, bitch. And you is as cheap as they comes.

Cee-Cee: I ain't cheap, mutha-fucker! Kiss my ass, you bitch. This ho's time is too precious to waste on a no-class, messed-up-from-the-chest-up, dope fiend like you. Get that big, ugly ass of yours outta my face. I'm sick of looking at ya.

LaTesha: Fuck you, bitch.

Cee-Cee: Fuck *you*, bitch!

And that was that. No more than ten minutes later they were exchanging commissary items and gossiping about a mutual acquaintance. A major deterrent to fighting was the write-up. There were two kinds of write-ups: majors and minors. You got a major for fighting, verbally assaulting a deputy, or destroying jail property. If you received a major, you would be punished with time, usually five days in "the hole." The hole was simply total isolation. The cell was the same as all the others, except that it had no window, no mirror and you couldn't see out the door. While in the hole, you could have only one pencil, no eraser, four pieces of writing paper, two envelopes, a toothbrush, comb, toothpaste, and a bible. No books or magazines, no razor, hairbrush, cup, commissary, cards, or anything else. In addition, a major meant automatic loss of your three-day-kick. No one does their full sentence. They do 2/3 of their sentence by law, and then get three days off of that due to overcrowding. Those who get a major write-up still only do 2/3 of their given sentence, but don't get the additional three days off. Minor write-ups, however, aren't so bad. You could get a minor for taking the newspaper from the dayroom into your cell, for not being up and ready for court, for not having your bra on while outside your cell, or a number of other minor rule violations. Punishment would just be loss of dayroom time and total confinement to your cell for a couple days. It was really no big deal except for people who liked to read the papers daily or who were coffee addicts, since the hot water was located in the dayroom. There were ways to get the hot water from the dayroom into a locked cell, however, so most ladies didn't even have to be without their coffee when being punished for a minor violation. We simply filled a cup with the hot water, slid a clean popcorn bag under the cell door and had the girl slide the opening of the bag in between the door and door jamb. We'd then fill her bag up by pouring the water into the opening and, consequently, through the door. With nothing but time on their hands, the inmates found ways around many, if not most, restrictions.

Money will determine whether the accused goes to prison or walks out of the courtroom a free man.

~Johnnie Cochran

4
PARKER'S PANTS, TRACY'S DOG, MEGHAN'S TAT AND EDWARD'S RELIGION – A TRIP TO COURT

One early morning while sitting in a dank basement holding cell with a group of other women waiting to be bussed to court, I noticed a bleach blonde girl twirling her hair compulsively around her finger and pacing every now and then. She refused to sit. She just stood and twirled, stood and twirled. When the time finally arrived to board the bus, we lined up along the wall and waited for our names to be called. Each of us was handcuffed to a partner. My name was called and I stepped forward. Parker was called and the still-twirling blonde stood beside me. She refused to sit once we boarded the bus, and attempted to be very casual about this. I asked, "Is something wrong? Why don't you relax a little?"

She glanced at me and quickly looked away. "No, I'm fine. Just a bit nervous."

"Are you looking at a pretty heavy case?" I inquired.

"Shoplifting."

"Your first time in jail?"

"No," she mumbled. "My fourth."

"Oh...all for shoplifting?"

"Uh huh."

And so went our fascinating conversation. When we arrived at the courthouse, we were immediately lined up in the hallway outside our holding cells, released from our cuffs and thoroughly patted down and searched for contraband. All we were allowed to bring to court was a bible – nothing else, not even an alternative book, a pencil, or piece of candy. The deputy marshal reached Parker and began her search. She ran her fingers through the twirled blonde hair. She checked inside the mouth. She ran her fingers around the bra straps and patted down the stomach. She laid her palm firmly against the crotch, and hesitated briefly. She lifted her eyes to meet the girl's, which were darting frantically about the room. The marshal gently touched the area again and then stepped abruptly back with a perplexed look on her face. "Uh, what…uh…" she stammered. "Jim, come over here, please." She waved the tall, bulky sergeant over and they conferred in private for a moment. I looked at Parker, but she was intently twirling again and appeared frightened, so I didn't know what to say. The two marshals promptly returned and the male was the first to speak. "Do you have anything that we should know about in your pants, Miss?"

The girl looked directly at him and said "What? No."

Then the female marshal spoke up. "I felt something. Could you tell me what I felt?"

"It's nothing, really. Uh…Ummmmm…It's just… it's just…a… banana."

The man broke out in laughter and told the female marshal, "I told you it wasn't! I told you. A banana! Ha-ha!"

"Take it out now," she demanded, trying to hold in her laughter. "Take it out and put it in that trash can." As Parker reached down and took the firm yellow fruit from its position in her underpants, the deputy marshal asked, "By the way, what pray tell are you doing with a banana in your panties?"

Parker hesitated for a moment before dropping the offending fruit into the can, then reluctantly responded, "I took it from breakfast this morning 'cause the court sack lunches aren't very filling and I end up starving every time I come."

A shoplifter who shoplifts from her own breakfast. Interesting. The searches continued and pencils, candy and other miscellaneous items were discovered and discarded, but no more bananas. After the search phase was over and we were all settled down in our large, cold, concrete holding cells, waiting to be called to appear, Parker finally had a seat and didn't touch her hair for the rest of the morning. I lost track of her in the confusion that day and never found out how much time she received for her fourth shoplifting charge. My name was called early and when I returned later, she was in another holding cell in a different part of the courthouse.

My appearance in court was merely for the sake of being officially present while the attorneys and the judge agreed on a trial date for my case. The path through our system of justice to an ultimate end of either conviction or exoneration is a long and arduous one filled with myriad hearings and conferences that require a defendant's presence. So when my name was called and I was ushered into the courtroom with a group of other equally-sedate women, I wasn't particularly tense or nervous, just drained and tired. I sat back and listened to the cases that were presented before mine. Just the usual: Drugs, prostitution, DUI, etc., until Tracy Russell was called forward. She was charged with bestiality after witnesses reported her having sex with a pit bull. When the man who owned the dog exited his house and saw what was happening on his lawn, he pulled Tracy away from the animal and immediately called police. She spent a short period of time in jail for that offense, but upon her release, she allegedly went back and committed the act again. She was now appearing in court for this repeat performance. The judge harshly reprimanded Tracy for not obeying his previous orders to leave the dog alone and urged her to seek help for her apparent problems. He finally said, "Miss Russell, I must inform you that the dog now has a restraining order against you, and that if you violate that order you can and will be returned to jail." This rabbit hole was becoming even more absurd than Alice's, and the show was becoming an intriguing distraction from my own problems and concerns. I felt grateful to Tracy for making me momentarily forget that my own world had crashed down around me. Hey, at least a dog didn't have a restraining order against me. Things could always be worse.

On my ride back to OCWJ that evening, I was handcuffed to an attractive girl named Meghan who was in for possession of heroin. A slender girl with long dark hair, olive skin, perfect fine features and deep brown eyes, she looked like she belonged in a high school drama club or soccer team, not shackled to me on a jail bus. We talked a lot and I grew to like her. She was 22, my age, and seemed to be very intelligent and keenly aware of the world around her. I was sad to learn that she had contracted AIDS through a dirty needle when she was 18 and was probably going to be dead within five years. She pulled the collar of her t-shirt down to reveal a tattoo printed under her collarbone in two-inch-high letters that read "Fuck The World." She said that's how she feels "about AIDS and the way it came about and how this world really is." She believed the government created the AIDS virus and could destroy it if it wanted to, but that it never would because the disease is being used as a method of population control. She was bitter, angry and hurt.

There was so little I could say, and my heart ached for her. Her parents had both been drug addicts and she was raised in the streets. Her intelligence and charm only got her so far when she was penniless and on her own, and she had to sell her body to survive – a cycle I saw repeated in virtually all of the prostitution cases. The waste of life and waste of truly amazing potential is beyond tragic. For the wealthiest country in the world to allow a substantial proportion of its citizens to live and die in the streets with virtually no protection or support is shameful, and is destroying innocent lives every day. Third-world conditions exist in many pockets of this nation, but these citizens often receive more disdain than compassion. Society sees their actions, but not the source of those actions, and that is one of the most significant obstacles to putting an end to the suffering and criminal activity. The public does not know of the hells that these women endure prior to partaking in a criminal life. They are degraded, demeaned, used, abused and treated like trash by those who are supposed to love them and teach them how to live in this world. Then society still expects them to live just as socially-appropriately as those raised in healthy, loving families. That is a ludicrous expectation; and further abusing people who do what they do *because* they were abused is not a solution to the problem. The United States needs to seriously re-examine its correctional policies and take a closer look at the value of actual efforts at rehabilitation rather than pure revenge-based punishment.

Sitting in front of Meghan and I on the bus in a caged seat was a tall, handsome, muscular young man clutching a bible. I spoke to him a bit and he eventually gave me his name, booking number and housing location so I could write to him. I looked at the name he had written – Edward Patrick Morgan – and quickly placed it. He had been arrested about a year earlier for raping and murdering a girl he met in a popular Orange County nightclub, and was facing the death penalty for his crime. He was caught on a security camera across the street from the club mercilessly beating and sexually assaulting her, then lying down beside her in a fetal position and eventually wandering away. He had prior rape convictions and had been recently paroled from prison. I was somewhat stunned when I realized who I had been talking to. Then I began to mentally review our conversation. He really only was interested in quoting verses from the bible and talking about the power of Jesus to change people's lives if they only devote themselves to him, heart and soul. Other than that, the only thing he said that could be construed as revealing came when I asked what sports he liked and if he cared for basketball. He said, "No, I hate basketball. My sports are wrestling and boxing. I'm an outrageous wrestler." He bragged about all the wrestling awards he had won and how competitive he was. I didn't find out much more about Edward Patrick Morgan through the letters he wrote as he was only interested in matters relating to religion and redemption. That's all he ever wrote about – nothing more.

There were always interesting people to meet on court days. Women and men rode the same busses since we were all handcuffed and the individual seats had cages around them, which made groping impossible. However, the cages didn't keep us from talking and exchanging names and booking numbers as well as information about our fellow inmates. On one occasion, a couple guys were picking on John Famalaro for being the biggest pack-rat they had ever seen. Famalaro was awaiting trial for abducting a young woman from an Orange County freeway shoulder where her car had broken down, killing her and leaving her body in a freezer outside his house in Arizona for three years before she was found. The men railed against him for taking things from the dayroom into his cell and never bringing them out again. They called his room the "black hole," because anything that went in never saw the light of day again. Apparently the entire place was packed with miscellaneous junk. The deputies would make him clean it out, but it would just get packed again as soon as they turned their backs.

Riding the bus from jail to court often felt more like going on a field trip with a bunch of obnoxious kids than going to face judgment with rapists, murderers, drug dealers and prostitutes. They were always laughing and joking and making fun of people in passing cars and walking on the sidewalk. Connections were established and plans were laid out for future crimes. Love connections were made and lewd innuendoes ran rampant. It was a bus full of the misfits of society who were despised and knew they were despised, but who for now were comfortable and fully accepted in the company of their own kind.

Prison makes you a better judge of character. You pick up on people much faster.

~Suge Knight

5
ANTOINETTE'S MYSTERIOUS VISITOR AND MARIA'S DILEMMA

An interesting individual who moved into Sector 14 a couple months after I had been there, but who had been arrested months earlier and placed in a different sector, was Antoinette Yancey. Antoinette was a 5'6", 120 pound, twenty-eight-year-old Black woman originally from Compton who was in on a death penalty case. She was charged with killing a twenty-four-year-old girl who was to testify against Yancey's boyfriend, who was being charged with murder. Antoinette's boyfriend and some friends robbed an electronics store, tied up the employees and placed them in a back room. When the men were exiting the store, they apparently came face-to-face with the 45-year-old mother of a 16-year-old boy who worked there and whom she had come to pick up. One of the men shot her in the head, killing her. The boyfriend and his cohorts were subsequently arrested and the twenty-four-year-old girl strengthened the case against them by testifying at a grand jury hearing that she had witnessed the murder and that the men charged were the ones she saw that night.

Shortly after the hearing, the girl was found shot once in the back of the head in a parking lot. Antoinette was among the suspects questioned, and when a gun fitting the description of the one used in the murder was discovered in her residence, she was arrested and brought to OCWJ.

Antoinette was mellow, reserved and quiet. She was very easy-going and good-natured, but had lived a difficult life growing up in Compton as the daughter of a single welfare mother who was also a drug addict. Antoinette had to steal money from her mother's purse to buy food for herself and her younger siblings. In spite of her harsh environment and detestable upbringing, she began working early in her life and wisely avoided the drug traps that snared so many of her peers. She excelled in school and graduated with a cumulative GPA of 3.8, which later assisted her in getting accepted to USC. Antoinette vehemently denied having any part in the murder of the girl, but even if she had, she would have known better than to admit it openly among the likes of us. No one was guilty. No one ever came in and said, "Yes, they're right, I did commit this crime." Denial is standard procedure in jail.

The most interesting aspect of Antoinette's case wasn't directly related to her, but to her constant and only visitor. He was a tall, middle-aged white businessman who was from an upper-middle class neighborhood in Mission Viejo. Every visiting day he was there. She was at OCWJ for almost two years, and he saw her, faithfully, every Friday, Saturday and Sunday. On Sunday mornings while waiting to be called, my mother and this man spoke about many things. One of those things was Antoinette's case. Her visitor revealed that he had only known Antoinette for three weeks before her arrest, but that, strangely, he was the one accepting full responsibility for all of her legal fees. In a year he had already spent over $100,000. He appeared nervous and extremely troubled about her fate. At one point, he told my mother about a couple possible exculpatory pieces of forensic data that could help the case tremendously if it wasn't discounted in some way by the prosecution. He said it had somehow been determined that the killer was taller than Antoinette and was left-handed. They sat and discussed the possible implications of such evidence in her case until they were called to their respective visits.

The next time they showed up, my mother observed that he signed in with his left hand. That day he revealed that he, too, had been questioned by the police a couple times. He said they wanted to get copies of his phone records, but that he retained a lawyer of his own and so they weren't going to get a thing out of him without a fight.

Although Antoinette was a white-bander, she was not in my dayroom group. She had to spend her dayroom time alone. Since her boyfriend allegedly used the phone to contact her to set up the hit, she was forbidden access to the dayroom phone for fear that she would do the same thing. Any time she was in the dayroom, the phones had to be off. However, we often sat and spoke to her through her door and learned that, whether she was guilty or not, she was a strong and resilient individual. She became the voice of reason in our sector, resolving any dispute with her flawless skills of logic. Yes, the hated became our friends – because we, too, were the hated.

Soon to be among us was Maria Martinez, the poverty-stricken Mexican farm worker who kidnapped toddler Stephanie Zamora from a Sears in Santa Ana and drove the child to her home in Delano. She had conned the baby's aunt into believing the girl was potential model material and that she, Maria, would pay her $500 to allow her to photograph the child. Maria sent the aunt on an errand to a distant part of the store while she waited with Stephanie. When the aunt returned, the two were gone. Bulletins went out on every news report and pictures of little Stephanie appeared in all the newspapers. A neighbor of Maria's saw one of these pictures while watching the news and recognized the child as the one Martinez had presented as her own. Maria had told her husband and friends that she had given birth to the child several months previous in Orange County, but that the girl had to remain hospitalized there for medical reasons. The neighbor who saw the news report called police and told them where to find their kidnapper. Stephanie was subsequently turned over to her parents and Maria was turned over to OCWJ.

Maria was a short, heavy-set woman in her late 30's with scraggly teeth and a thick accent. She spoke primarily in Spanish and spent the vast majority of her time grouped with the other Spanish-speaking inmates. However, when she did socialize with the rest of us, she was openly accepted as though she had been with us the whole time. She said she had stolen the baby because she had recently had a miscarriage while in Mexico and feared that she would never be able to have children of her own. She couldn't think of a response when we asked why she didn't consider the parents' feelings when she took their child away. She would only look around dumbly and shrug her shoulders. That wasn't a concern of hers at the time, nor was it a concern of hers now. All she was worried about was how much time she was going to get.

Before one of Maria's court dates, she asked if I would cut her hair, and I agreed. When an inmate needed a haircut, they requested approval to have a fellow inmate use the scissors in the presence of a deputy. For some reason, I was selected for this duty quite frequently. While I snipped at Maria's hair, she related to me a dilemma she was facing. She had become very interested in a guy from the men's jail whom she had met on the bus on the way to an earlier court appearance. They had written extensively and the attraction by both parties continued to grow. When the man got released, he became a runner for her and put money in her commissary account on several occasions. The problem was, both her husband and this man were going to be in court the next day to see her and she was a bit fearful. Her husband didn't have any knowledge of this other man, and she was concerned about what might happen if Mr. Martinez were to notice the connection between the two. She giggled and squealed like a teen-aged girl about the possibilities. I told her she was surely better off dumping her new love and sticking by her husband the way he was sticking by her. Her only response was, "But Jennifer, he's sooooooo cute," and then another giggle.

The big day came and passed drama-free. Maria managed to acknowledge and wink at both husband and boyfriend without either being the wiser.

ORANGE COUNTY WOMEN'S JAIL

Jail is much easier on people who have nothing.

~Bernhard Goetz

6
DEBBIE DOES DAYROOM AND CEE-CEE'S SECRETS

Standing at our doors for daily head-count at 5 a.m. one bright morning shortly after Christmas and New Years, the girl in the cell to my left demanded from the deputy in the dayroom, "Hey deputy. Am I fat?" The deputy looked the girl over and finally said, "Why are you asking me?"

"Because," she retorted. I need an objective opinion. If you had never seen me before now, would you think I looked fat?"

The deputy glared at the chubby miscreant once more, rolled her eyes, and began walking to the next sector. The girl, now irritated, bellowed, "Damn, can't even get a straight answer around here! This place sucks."

And so began one of the first days of 1995 in Sector 14. The girl, Debbie, a 36-year-old hyperactive annoyance of sorts, was in on paraphernalia charges and was none too pleased with her surroundings. She was another regular at OCWJ, always getting arrested during the chilly winter months. She joined Ardith, Cee-Cee and myself for a little gin rummy or spades from time to time, and always kept our attention with her uniquely creative imagination. Her tales abounded with references to rich and famous individuals who were supposedly close friends of hers. According to Debbie, Hulk Hogan was her boyfriend a few years back before she dropped him to date Arsenio Hall's drug connection. She explained in erratic and inconsistent detail how Mr. Hogan had become despondent after she gave him the news and continued to pursue her to that day. Debbie said she also was a close friend of Dean Koontz, whom she claimed would periodically take her for rides along the Coast Highway 1 near Malibu on the back of his Harley Davidson motorcycle. Speaking of vehicles, she tried to sell me a five-year-old car with no defects for a mere $800. She said it was a must-sell situation and she simply had to get rid of it. I soon discovered that it was the car of an acquaintance of hers who was also in jail at the time and who therefore wouldn't miss it for a few months. We all sat and listened to her ludicrous yarns in a state of dumbstruck silence until Cee-Cee just couldn't take it anymore. "Ya know what, bitch," she snarled. "If you think we buy one half of the crock you been feedin' us, you bes' just check yourself, 'cause you got another thing comin'."

"What? You think I'm lying? Is that it? You're calling me a liar?" Debbie vainly protested.

"Bingo, babe," Cee exclaimed. "But that's not the bad thing. The bad thing is that you're such a God-damn shitty fuckin' liar. If you must do it, at least have the fuckin' sense to do it well."

Ardith began tittering and rocking back and forth in her seat, covering her mouth with her hands to contain the laughter. I cracked half a smile and pretended to be concentrating on my cards and the game.

"This is bullshit," Debbie cried. "I don't have to take this crap from anyone. You bunch of weirdoes can play without me if that's how you feel. Fuck! This place sucks!"

"By the way," added Cee-Cee, "To answer the question you asked the deputy this morning, you're fuckin' fat as a pig."

Debbie marched off to a distant table in a huff and sat down with a group of unsuspecting victims. The entire time she spent in jail, she never found a niche, which was likely the case in the outside, as well. We all had our own problems; we didn't have the time or patience for someone else's make-believe problems.

Later that day when Ardith was in the bathroom having a typical flatulence uproar and all the others were walking around the perimeter of the dayroom for exercise, Cee-Cee and I had an interesting conversation. Somewhere along the way the street-tough inflections disappeared from her speech, as did the vulgarities that seemed so much a part of her character. She talked about her past and speculated about her future. She was not the same person I had known the past six months. She was a woman I could have come across in the park with her kids, or could have met in class as a college student. She told me that she grew up an only child in Washington state. Although her father was a busy psychiatrist, she received all of his attention. Unfortunately, it wasn't the kind of attention she wished to receive. Beginning when she was about 9 or 10, he began visiting her room in the middle of the night while his wife slept to molest her. It started out with just fondling, then progressed. He asked her to play with him and said that it would "make daddy very happy." As time went by, the man desired more and more out of their surreptitious meetings. Fondling progressed to oral sex, which progressed to intercourse. Eventually, her father didn't even bother to try to hide his acts from his wife, and would initiate sex with Cee-Cee just before bedtime – sometimes as a prelude to sex with her mother. Finally, when she was 14, she became pregnant by her father. By now she knew what they were doing was wrong. She despised the man with a passion, and didn't particularly care for her mother considering she had allowed the abuse to happen and never tried to protect her. The parents wanted her to get an abortion, but Cee-Cee had other plans. She fled the state and ran away to California with an older boy, Ted, who had recently graduated from their high school.

Cee-Cee gave birth to a son and immediately put him up for adoption. To make some extra money Ted began sending her out on the streets to turn tricks. She quickly established a reputation and had a number of regulars who supplied her with a steady income. It was one of these regulars who introduced her to the drug scene, which she then introduced to Ted. Ted quickly developed a taste for crack cocaine and it eventually became his favorite source of personal entertainment. Cee-Cee enjoyed drugs, but could take them or leave them. She never really became an addict, as many prostitutes do. Ted continued acting as her pimp to support his habit and to provide her with a place to stay so she wouldn't have to return to Washington. Cee-Cee was quite pleased when the counterfeiting scheme proved to be lucrative, since it meant her days as a prostitute were over. She finally felt a glimmer of hope – the possibility of a real, decent life was now within her reach. She said she imagined herself living alone in the country with just a couple of cats, a dog, and not a soul around for miles.

As we discussed her modest dreams, I was somewhat surprised and very pleased to learn that she hadn't abandoned them. She wasn't deterred by the fact that their master plan had fallen through; she was still determined. "Look at all the people out there who do it legally," she said. "If they can do it, I can." She told me she had once enrolled for classes at a local junior college after getting her GED while in jail, but felt so out of place that she just couldn't handle it. "I honestly tried," she said. "But you just don't know what it's like when you have absolutely nothing in common with the other students. You can't make conversation. You can't make friends. When I'd go back to my 'hood, I was comfortable again – it was the only place I felt accepted and like I really belonged."

Cee-Cee said that if Ted did his part and said in their trial that she had nothing to do with his drug or counterfeiting activities and she got to go free, she would re-enroll at that same JC and stick with it this time. She said that Ted's long-term incarceration would give her the chance to finally just think about herself and her own best interests.

As the deputies came over the speakers to announce the conclusion of our dayroom time, I realized what a unique individual the person I had been talking to was. Something in her resolve told me that Cee-Cee could accomplish anything she set her mind to, and I was sure she would someday have the life she wished for.

JENNIFER SWEET

In jail I was just like everybody else;

I was sitting there praying, feeling caged.

~Dennis Rodman

7
LATESHA

LaTesha was another of OCWJ's frequent flyers. At 5'4" and about 280 pounds with a mouth, voice and attitude to match her body, LaTesha was impossible to miss. She was a thirty-eight-year-old African American woman and proud prostitute. In the two years I spent incarcerated, LaTesha was released and rearrested three times. She once told me that out of the last ten years, she had spent a combined seven incarcerated. We met when I sat down at her table for dinner in the dayroom shortly after her most recent arrival. Before formal introductions, she gave me the low-down: "I don't know wha choo doin' here, lil' white girl, and it ain't none of my business, but I tell you straight right here and now, I the biggest, bestest ho this side of Tallahassee, and I ain't afraid to say it!"

Picking up on her sense of humor, I responded, "That's quite an accomplishment. You must be very proud."

LaTesha dropped her plastic spoon into her spaghetti and ceased chewing while she stared intently at me. Finally, she very calmly and seriously said, "Damn right I am," as a greasy noodle slid out of her mouth and onto her considerable lap. She shoved another spoonful of jail slop into her mouth before even chewing the first and spewed bits of noodle and meat back into her plate as she said to me, "Fuck yeah! Those mens ain't wantin' no skinny, sucked-up hos. They think they all gots AIDS 'n shit. They look at me and they *knows* I'm a healthy ho. I got mens standin' in line waitin' for a piece of my sweet cheeks."

Losing my appetite after seeing more half-chewed spaghetti dribble down her chin, I pushed my tray aside and responded: "Well, now that I think about it, you're probably right. In this day and age, I would imagine the thin girls would scare a lot of men away with just the possibility that they could be infected. Business must be booming for you."

This was LaTesha's cue to stuff her face even more and gleefully tell me in great detail how tricks would drive right past the skinny girls every time and pull up beside her for a "date." She said the first time she ever turned a trick was when her girlfriend turned her onto it in her mid-twenties. She was terrified, but the friend assured her it was nothing but easy money. When the first man propositioned her, she initially declined, but his begging and pleading made her feel guilty, so she got into his car. He was a middle-aged businessman in a late-model foreign car. She was scared to death when he drove to a dark alley and instructed her to turn around in the front seat and take her pants down, but she mechanically followed his orders. The next thing she knew, his hand was gently rubbing and massaging her expansive backside. She then realized his other hand was being used to service his penis. When he was through, he gave her $20, said thank you and left. LaTesha was elated. Her friend had said it was easy, but she had no idea it would be this easy. She told me that she frequently was paid for performing acts such as that first one that weren't even sexual (on her part). For example, she had a regular who liked her to sit in his car and rev the engine while he stood on the front bumper with the hood open, masturbating into it. Another trick received his greatest pleasure from sitting on the floor across from her, both of them naked, and rolling grapefruits back and forth into each other's open legs. That particular service was worth $50.

LaTesha was very amusing. She talked tough, but we knew she was a big teddy bear underneath it all. She had a beautiful, bright smile, and when she walked she waddled like a giant todler. Her humor was relentless and you never had to worry about dishonesty with her – she's one of the few who would always tell it like it is. Everyone loved LaTesha, and she loved everyone. We all saved some of our butter from breakfast for her, which she used as grease for her hair. No matter how often we told her that it simply smelled rancid, she continued to use it. "Death before nappy hair" was her mantra. When Debbie would begin one of her numerous tall tales, LaTesha would swiftly raise her hand in the air and say, "Debbie, Debbie, Debbie, don't even start with that bullshit of yours. Ain't nobody in the mood for it and ain't nobody gonna believe it anyways. So just save your breath, sweetheart."

About five years earlier, LaTesha and her boyfriend, who also served as her pimp, got into one of their typical intense screaming matches. This particular fight was regarding his share of her earnings – an old and familiar source of tension between them. Jerome accused her of holding out on him and threatened to throw LaTesha and their one-year-old son out of their rodent-ridden apartment and into the streets if she didn't start handing over a considerable amount more than what she had been. They were outside on the sidewalk when he repeated one of his favorite new catchphrases and began walking away: "Bitch, ya best ho up and not slow up, then kick the dough up when ya show up."

This degrading remark, in addition to the countless others that preceded it, was the proverbial straw that broke the camel's back. LaTesha had finally reached her breaking point. She ran across the street to their '76 Chevrolet, started the engine and went roaring in Jerome's direction. With his final words replaying in her mind, she jumped the curb and cut the man down before he had a chance to react. He became lodged in the rear axle and was dragged for 80 feet before dropping off. At this point, LaTesha did a quick 180 and ran over his lifeless prostrate body once more. Jerome was dead. He had numerous broken bones, a broken neck and massive internal injuries. LaTesha was brought to trial and ultimately given 7 years in prison for manslaughter. Whereas in Orange County jail an inmate actually only really serves 2/3 of her sentence, in prison an inmate only serves ½ of her sentence, so LaTesha was free once again after 3 ½ years. I asked her if she felt badly about what she had done and she said, "Hell no! I just wish I'd done it sooner. That asshole used to beat the fuck outta me, night and day. It was about time for him to get a lil' taste of his own medicine, if you know what I means."

It sounds kind of strange, but jail time was almost a good experience for me.

~Tommy Lee

8
ROOF REC

On one unusually hot spring day, all the white-banders from Sector 14 went to roof rec (roof recreation) to enjoy the warmth of the sun and get some fresh air. Roof rec was the only time we were allowed to go outside, and we only got that opportunity two times a week for an hour each time. It wasn't even actually outside. It was an 80' x 50' space inside high brick walls on the roof of our building, with a basketball hoop and volleyball net with which we were to entertain ourselves. There was no grass; just cement ground and brick walls. We couldn't see trees or people or anything, only walls and sky, but that was better than nothing. We were grateful for what little we got.

On this particular day, no one wanted to play volleyball or basketball. We all just wanted to lie around in the sun and fresh air and talk about all the decadent foods we were going to eat when we got out. Debbie was there walking around the perimeter of the roof in an effort to lose some of that which made her chubby. She was intensely orating to a virgin who appeared to be in awe of what she was hearing. No one bothered to warn the newbie about Debbie's story-telling proclivities, as we felt that it would do her some good to figure it out on her own. Besides, we had better things to do; like lie in the sun and inhale and exhale. LaTesha was right there with us in spite of her already deep tan. So were Cee-Cee, Ardith and Myra. Whitney had done her time and had been released. Ardith spoke to me at length about her latest aches and pains, and even asked me if I would cut a small, insignificant mole off her neck with a razor because she was just positive it had to be cancer. I told her she should have the jail doctor check it out and let him decide what measures to take. She then moaned in exasperation and said she had already gone that route but that he said it was nothing but a harmless mole. She, of course, knew better and was determined to remove that malignancy from her personage one way or another. When I told her I didn't think I had the stomach to cut a mole off, she began to pout and punished me with the silent treatment.

As she arose to leave me to wrestle with my guilt for being so insensitive, I felt a cold, wet blob splat on my bare belly just centimeters below where I had my t-shirt tucked under my bra. When I opened my eyes, I saw our dearest Cee-Cee leaning high over me with a sly smirk on her face and a hand resting on her hip. "How do ya like me now?!" she teased. Looking down, I saw a large lump of wet toilet paper resting firmly upon my solar plexus. I could hear Ardith's tittering and LaTesha's cackle as well as the laughter of everyone else present, including Debbie and the virgin. "How do I like you now?" I asked, slowly rising to my feet. "I'll show you how I like you now, bitch." I then sprinted over to the water fountain, grabbed the toilet paper and made two quick water balls. I chased Cee all around the roof and finally nailed her on the right side of her head by her neck; then I catapulted the second one straight to her butt and said, "How do ya like *me* now?" By this time, several of the others had made water balls of their own and were chasing us mercilessly in that confined area. There was no escape. In the end, everyone had gotten in on the action and by the time the deputies saw us and demanded that we "knock it off," we were all soaking wet with bits of toilet paper clinging to our hair and clothes. It's surprisingly difficult to remove wet toilet paper from one's hair – take my word for it. The only person to complain afterward, however, was LaTesha. She would have to wash her hair and wouldn't have any butter for it for the rest of the day.

As we meandered back to our cells in Sector 14, dripping as we went, the blue-banders peered at us longingly. They wouldn't get to go to the roof until the following day, and who knew what the weather would be like by that time.

Every single person in jail for a violent crime had a nightmare childhood.

~Rob Reiner

9
LINDA AND THE WEED WHACKER

I awoke early one morning to the sound of an unfamiliar voice hurling a colorful variety of threats and accusations. The voice possessed a distinct English accent. The next thing I knew, Cee-Cee was yelling at me to go to my "phone." Our phones were the speakers in our rooms through which the deputies spoke to us. If you spoke at an average volume into your speaker, anyone in any cell in the sector could hear you clearly by placing their ear against their own speaker. The phone system was generally used early in the morning or late at night when screaming through the vents (another method of communication) would have disturbed fellow inmates' sleep. So, I answered my phone and listened for Cee. "Hey, Jen, do you hear that crazy bitch? She's two doors down from me, but sounds like she's behind my fuckin' vent. Shit, man, get a load of that broad. She's fuckin' spun!."

I focused my full attention on the accented syllables flowing from the foreigner's cell. "Spit it out...spit it out... I can't hear you, Jerry. Ohhh! You make me so angry. If you're not going to bail me out, then take your damn penis out of me! (beat) What? What? Oh, spit-it-out! It's that fucking tart, isn't it, Jerry! She's the reason you won't bail me out. You can have that evil, demonic, possessed, Satanist bitch. So just take your fucking penis out of me right this minute. (beat) What? What? I can't hear you. Spit it out, already!"

For the rest of the morning we were subjected to numerous variations on this same theme. Interestingly enough, no one yelled at her to shut up. We were all straining to hear what Jerry would do next to piss the woman off.

When we finally came out for dayroom at 8 a.m., all eyes turned to the thin, dark-haired woman who had provided our entertainment for the morning. The 40ish woman casually zipped her sweat jacket all the way up, kicked her cell door closed, sat down at the nearest table, decisively crossed her arms and legs, glanced around at our gawking faces, and said in her refined English accent, "What? What are you all staring at me for?"

Cee-Cee was the first to speak. "Where's Jerry?"

"Jerry? What do you mean? I don't know any Jerry," she barked defensively.

"Oh, sure you do... you know the Jerry who wouldn't 'spit it out' this morning, and who had a problem getting his penis out of you."

The English woman sat and glared at Cee-Cee in genuine horror. "You are a sick and mad individual. Please take your profanities elsewhere."

"Where the fuck do you get off callin' me sick, bitch?! You're the dumb mutha-fucker talkin' to the fuckin' walls. Kiss my ass, bitch. You ain't got a damn thing on me. Everybody here done heard you, too, ya crazy fuck," Cee-Cee yelled as she walked away. "Fuck this shit. I ain't got the time."

Everyone else followed Cee-Cee's lead and wandered off to their usual places around the room. I sat down across from the English woman and began playing solitaire. "Would you like to play cards?" I asked, trying to sound as non-threatening as possible.

"No. No, I wouldn't," she replied, giving me a discerning look. "What on earth is the matter with that girl?" she asked, referring to Cee-Cee. Why did she attack me with those hideous lies?"

"Well," I said, frantically searching for something inoffensive to say. "I really can't speak for anyone else. That's something you would have to address with her."

"But I never heard of anything so ludicrous in my life. She simply must be insane. She simply must. Is everyone in here as crazy as her?"

"No, actually most are more crazy. But you get used to it after a while. What's your name?" I inquired, trying to change the subject.

"Linda. What's yours?"

"Jennifer," I responded, extending a hand. "It's very nice to meet you, Linda. This your first time in jail?"

"Yes, and last. How about you?"

"My first, and last, time, too. I've been in a little over eight months now. Trust me. It's not as bad as you've heard; and it gets easier after a while."

"Eight months seems like a long time."

"It is if the time is wasted. But if you take advantage of the opportunities it offers to catch up on reading or to learn things you never had time for in the past, it doesn't seem that long. So what brought you here?" I asked.

"Oh!" she exclaimed. "It's that fucking ex-husband of mine! He had me arrested for violating a restraining order that I most certainly did not violate," she said with indignation. "That fucking Jerry... I just know this all has something to do with that cheap hussy he's been bedding who's really..."

"Jerry?" I interrupted. "Did you say your ex's name was Jerry?"

"Yes, that is what I said," she retorted impatiently.

"Wait a second. I'm confused. You told Cee-Cee you didn't know anyone by that name. What's going on?"

"Oh, I told her that because I recognized immediately that she was one of them," she said conspiratorially.

"One of who?"

"One of Jerry's spies. He plants them wherever I go. Did you see how angry she got when she realized I had found her out?" Linda grinned slyly and let a giggle slip through her lips.

"Yes, well... that's very interesting," I said, marveling at how similar her paranoid delusions were to Ardith's.

"You see, I'm psychic and Jerry's psychic and I could tell immediately that that girl was, too. He psychically wills his people to watch me and report my every move back to him. He's so silly, though, that he forgets that my own psychic powers tell me when another psychic is near," she continued.

"You're right," I agreed. "That is pretty silly of him. Is he aware that you, too, have psychic powers, or does he just think you're totally in the dark?"

"Oh, well of course he knows of my powers. We communicate through them all the time. We send messages back and forth day and night, no matter how far apart we are," she said.

"Is that right?"

"Yes, yes, it is. The only problem now is this new wench he's poking. Nothing but a tramp," she sneered. "All that's ever on his mind now is sex, sex, sex, and it's simply impossible to get him to focus his attention long enough to relay a coherent thought to me. It really pisses me off to no end, and it's all her fault," she cried.

"Well, uh…" I muttered. "How did all of this lead you here? In what way does he claim you violated the restraining order?"

"Oh," she sighed. "It's just too silly. I don't even want to talk about it."

"Okay," I said, with a sense of relief.

"The old fool had the nerve to tell the officers that I broke into his house in the middle of the night and snuck into what used to be our bedroom. It's alleged that when I discovered his hussy lying there beside him, I went into a rage, ran to the garage, came back and assaulted the both of them with a weed whacker. Isn't that the most absurd thing you've ever heard in your life?!" she said in almost a scream.

"Yes, yes. I would say it definitely is," I responded, just trying to stay on her good side.

"I mean, think about it. I'm psychic for Christ-sake. I'm not surprised by *anything*. Simply ridiculous."

"Well, was anyone injured?" I ventured.

"Oh, the little tart suffered some minor cuts and bruises, but nothing serious," she snarled.

"So, if you didn't do it, then how did she get cut up?"

Linda leaned close to me and said in a low, matter-of-fact tone, "You know, I wouldn't put it past the likes of her to use that weed whacker on herself just to see me rot behind bars."

"Sounds like a very sick woman," I said, recalling Ardith's similar conspiracy theory about her husband, her bordello client and her ex-lover framing her.

"Sick, sick, sick," she added.

After a lengthy pause, I inquired, "So, how's your case look? I mean, what's your attorney think your chances are?"

A wide grin stretched across her face and little laugh lines deepened at the corners of her eyes. "Oh, I've got a wonderful attorney," she cooed. "I was very lucky. I got a public defender who's also psychic."

I steadied myself for what was to come. "Well, isn't that nice?" I said.

"Oh yes. She has out-of-body experiences while we're in court and goes around the room giving blow jobs to the D.A. and judge and other male attorneys. She does this while they're in the midst of trying to build their case against me, so they get so excited and distracted that they mess up and forget things. Then she returns to her body and winks at me. I know what that wink means. I look around the room and all the men's pants have damp spots in front and they're bumbling like children," she said, then roared with laughter. "No, Jennifer, I don't think I have to worry about a thing where this case is concerned. I'll probably be out of here by next week."

Linda chuckled to herself and sat with her own thoughts for a while, which was a welcome break for me. Moments later, I slowly got up and excused myself to ostensibly use the restroom while she continued to giggle and moan in response to the mysterious images that were bouncing around inside her head. Early every morning we continued to hear her ordering Jerry to take his penis out of her if he wasn't going to bail her out, but none of the other psychics present made the mistake of bringing it to her attention ever again.

One afternoon I observed Ardith speaking at length to Linda. I thought, "Now that should make for an interesting friendship: a woman who believes she can communicate psychically with people, and one who believes an implant in her brain is transmitting her private thoughts to others. Surprisingly enough, Ardith walked over to me later that day and whispered, "That woman is weird."

Psychiatric disorders were commonplace at OCWJ, and treatment was so lacking that it was almost nonexistent. Although some of the encounters with the mentally ill were amusing on the outside, these were people who were suffering tremendously and who lived in very scary, lonely worlds. I, and most of the inmates, tried to show them compassion and understanding. In writing about my more light-hearted encounters with very troubled inmates, I do not seek to make fun of or denigrate them. They were all very resilient and strong people, despite their extremely difficult paths, and I would never put them down in such a way. We all, mentally ill and otherwise, did and said ridiculous things. Finding and focusing on the humor rather than on the pervasive tragedy was a survival mechanism that we all utilized.

America has the longest prison sentences in the West, yet the only condition long sentences demonstrably cure is heterosexuality.

~Bruce Jackson

10
JAIL LESBIANISM

One common stereotype regarding women in jail is that lesbianism runs rampant. That was half true and half not true at OCWJ. A great deal of homosexual activity occurs, but few of those involved would actually define themselves as lesbians. They're undoubtedly heterosexual, but because of the circumstances, if they experience sexual urges they can only look to other females to satisfy them. Most of these interactions only involved groping, massaging, intimate touching and hugging and kissing in the dayroom. But there were those occasions when such behavior escalated into full sexual encounters.

Quite common was the practice of romantically pursuing naïve virgins who were known to have good runners. To seduce and win the affections of such a girl was to be set-up with commissary for the rest of one's stay. Myra was one of the more aggressive pursuers and had a particular affinity for cute, feminine girls. She found the requisite qualities in the personage of a girl named Kori. Kori was twenty-six-years-old, about 5'5" and 120 pounds with blue eyes and straight blonde hair. She was a real estate agent whose biggest character flaw was naiveté. Kori was obviously flattered by Myra's attentions. Although Myra never so much as made it to first base with her, the one-way relationship ruffled a few feathers. There were those who were jealous of Kori and who consequently tried to woo Myra away from her. One individual in particular was Debbie. Debbie would walk up behind Myra and whisper inconsequential things in her ear as an excuse to rest her breasts on Myra's back. Myra would allow Debbie to sit on her lap with only one rule to the game: If Debbie told even one of her infamous tall tales, she would be banished from Myra's affections forever. Surprisingly enough, it worked. Debbie continued to be a pathological liar; just not when Myra was near.

The problem was, Debbie knew that while Myra's hands were fondling her ample bosoms, her eyes and thoughts were on Kori. So when Kori expressed a desire to have her hair trimmed, Debbie eagerly volunteered, saying she used to be a licensed beautician. Kori fell for the ruse and signed up for Sunday haircuts. You were only allowed to have your hair cut by someone from your dayroom group, and the scissors were only available on Sunday evenings, to be used under strict supervision, of course.

So when the big day came and Debbie stood poised over Kori's unsuspecting head with the sharp instruments in her hand, we all looked on in anticipation of what the alleged former beautician would do next.

There's a subtle difference between a trim and a cut. Apparently that's a difference Debbie didn't learn in beauty school. Kori had medium-length hair to begin with; about to her shoulders. But now it couldn't be mistaken for anything but a short bob. All throughout the ordeal, Kori kept chirping, "Not too much, now. Just a little trim." But words were meaningless to Debbie. She was a woman with a mission: Make the competition as ugly as possible to win the woman of her dreams. It might have worked had Myra been the superficial type of recreational lesbian, but she wasn't. She continued to make out with Debbie while lavishing her most erotic and sincere compliments on Kori.

Unbeknownst to Myra, Debbie and the rest of the sector, Kori was already involved in an exclusive private affair with Cee-Cee. They, unlike everyone else, weren't into public displays of affection, and shared their intimacies out of the view of others.

Kori was arrested for allegedly hiring a hit man to kill her boyfriend after he broke up with her. He had been having an affair with a close friend of hers for a couple of months prior to the break-up, which only served to add to the grief and pain she was experiencing. She spoke candidly to me about her predicament. She, like LaTesha, reached what she termed "a breaking point" when she saw him in the market holding hands and nuzzling the other woman. Despite the fact that she and her boyfriend were separated, it still felt to Kori like he was cheating on her. Her love for him carried on while his love was shamelessly directed toward another. Kori contacted an old friend whom she knew to be involved in shady operations and asked for an estimate on this job she wanted done. The friend gave her a reference and instructed her to phone the man, Michael, later that evening. The call was made and the bidding war began. Michael wanted $10,000 but Kori insisted she couldn't go a dime over $5,000. Mike went soft in the end and agreed to make the hit for $5,500.

Kori met and paid Michael the initial $3,000 and a week later, after her boyfriend was found dead with a single bullet wound to the back of his head, she presented Mike with the remaining $2,500. She was arrested six months later when Mike was arrested on a separate charge and linked to the murder and, ultimately, to her. When I left OCWJ (after two years), Kori was still awaiting trial, but she was facing life and it didn't look good. In the meantime, Myra's attention and Cee-Cee's affection were taking her mind off her terrible deed and ultimate fate.

ORANGE COUNTY WOMEN'S JAIL

You can jail a Revolutionary, but you can't jail the Revolution.

~Huey Newton

11
DANA ALLMAN

Cee-Cee and I were playing chess when a strange new inmate named Dana was released into our zoo. A skinny girl with long, wild, blonde hair, she tossed her bedroll into her cell, shut the door, spun around on her heals, threw her arms in the air and said, "How ya'all doin'? My name's Dana Allman." She walked briskly toward each person, arm extended for a tight handshake. "My daddy's Gregg Allman, with the Allman Brothers Band, and I'm just mighty damn glad to meet ya'all." She broke into song and danced wistfully about the room. Then she stopped and sat at a table occupied by LaTesha, Myra and Kori and said admiringly to LaTesha, "My, you're a big ole gal, ain't ya?"

"Fly away, lil' white girl, befo' I makes you fly," snarled LaTesha.

"Ha-ha! You're a trip!" Dana squealed and patted LaTesha on the back as she leapt to her feet and began singing once more. She sashayed over to the wall speaker by the dayroom entrance door and, still singing at the top of her lungs, pushed the little red button that is not to be touched except in medical emergencies. "What is your medical emergency?" demanded Deputy Stonefeld through the speaker.

"Medical emergency? Ha-ha. I ain't got no medical emergency. No ma'am. I just wanna ask ya..."

"The button is for medical emergencies only. If you aren't dying, then get away from the speaker," Stonefeld warned contemptuously.

Dana moved a little to the right of the speaker and began making elaborate motions in the air with her hands and arms in the direction of the deputy's pod.

"What are you doing now?" Deputy Stonefeld asked.

"Oh, well, I was talkin' sign language to ya'. Since ya'all can't talk to me through the speaker, I thought ya might at least talk in sign language," Dana responded cheerfully.

"What's your problem?" Stonefeld asked.

"Oh, I ain't got no problem, ma'am. I was just wonderin' if ya'all could tell me what time it is, 'cause we ain't got no clocks in here, that's all." Dana turned her big blonde head around and gave us a sly wink.

"What do you need the time for; you got a date?" Stonefeld barked.

"Ha-ha! That's a good one," Dana cried, doubling over in faux laughter. "But seriously," she said. "I gotta know 'cause Daddy Gregg's got a gig tonight and I've gotta get ahold of him before he leaves so he can come on down here and bail me outta this place. That's all, miss deputy."

"Go away," came the reply through the speaker.

"What? You ain't gonna tell me what time it is?"

"Go away."

"But I'm Dana Allman. My daddy's Gregg Allman with the Allman Brothers Band, and I gotta know what time it is so I can tell Daddy Gregg before he leaves."

"You're lying. Go away, go away, go away," the deputy said.

It was apparent that deputy Stonefeld had had enough and wasn't going to comply with Dana's request. Dana whipped around, pointed to the speaker and said, "Did ya'all hear that? That ole gal wouldn't even give me the time. Daddy Gregg'll get a kick outta that one. Wooo-weee!" She picked up her unidentifiable song where she had left off and bounced around in her own little world. Cee-Cee yelled, "Hey, you crazy bitch! Why don't you shut that big trap before I put somethin' in it? You're pissin' everybody off with the 'Daddy Gregg' shit, so save the drag."

Raising her hands in mock surrender and maintaining her broad, beaming grin, Dana replied: "Hey, no problem, homegirl. I'm hip to what you're sayin'. It's cool, it's cool."

"Damn straight, ho. You bes' just watch your step 'cause I ain't no homegirl of yours and never will be. Just keep it outta my space and ever lil' thang'll be just skippy."

Dana was in for trespassing and assault on a bail bondsman. She had waltzed off the street into the ballroom of a local upscale hotel where a private gala was taking place, plopped herself down at the empty piano bench, and announced herself as the entertainment for the evening. She told the awed crowd that "Daddy Gregg" couldn't make it that night, but that he sent his love to one and all. She began awkwardly slapping away at the piano keys and asked for requests before she broke out in loud, incomprehensible song. Finally, to everyone's relief, the manager and a couple of burly security guards came and diplomatically escorted her to the lobby. She put up a fight when they attempted to deposit her back onto the street and screamed, "But my fans, my fans! I can't let them down!" Dana already had a warrant out for her arrest for a prior drug charge which was discovered once she got to the station. She called a bail bondsman to come bail her out. When he arrived and asked for his money, she refused to give it up, saying, "Just put it on Daddy Gregg's tab." The man didn't appreciate her sense of humor and turned to leave. "No!" Dana cried, "You can't leave me here!" She grabbed his jacket tail through the bars of the holding cell and pulled him close.

"Let go of me, you nut," he said, trying to free himself from her grip.

"Ha-ha. I ain't no nut, sir. I'm a singer. My daddy's Gregg Allman of the Allman Brothers Band and his credit is good. Trust me!" Dana pulled forcefully on the man's jacket and he stumbled forward, smashing his nose against one of the iron bars. Blood spurt out and onto Dana's face. She finally released her grip. The man's nose was broken and, of course, he was pressing charges.

Dana kept us all entertained for several months to come with her antics. Among other things, she was a veritable nudist. We had one curtained shower on the upper tier of the sector and one downstairs on the first floor. Every other day she walked stark naked, towel around her head, to and from the shower, singing away like a sick and dying bird. She never wore a stitch of clothes while in her cell and startled deputies on numerous occasions when they walked by while she was in the midst of performing high-energy exercises. But of all the crazy things she did, only one unforgivable act turned the entire sector against her. She killed Elvis. We had a mouse that would always come out at night and nibble on the little scraps we had dropped during meals. Occasionally, he would even crawl under our doors and sniff around our rooms. He was a mouse, a pet, a friend. Late one fateful night, little Elvis made the tragic mistake of entering the room of the wild nude woman. When she heard him scratching at her trash bag, she reflexively grabbed a shower shoe and flung it in the direction of the sound. All was quiet. The following morning, Dana discovered our friend deep in a state of rigor mortis. The poor guy had died of a heart attack, and our sector fell into a state of mourning for our lost companion.

ORANGE COUNTY WOMEN'S JAIL

Three hundred years ago a prisoner condemned to the Tower of London carved on the wall of his cell this sentiment: It is not adversity that kills, but the impatience with which we bear adversity.

~James Keller Quotes

12
GOODBYES

Cee-Cee returned from a court hearing absolutely ecstatic. Through a plea-bargain arrangement, Ted had pled guilty to all charges in exchange for a reduced sentence and cleared her of having any role in the counterfeiting and drug crimes. Cee-Cee was going home. When we came out for our second dayroom that night, she was just waiting for the paperwork to go through so she could be released. Everything was packed and she kept an ear to the speaker in anticipation of hearing her name called that one last time. She was happier than I had ever seen her. She bounced around the dayroom laughing like a little girl on her birthday.

Everyone understood. Things had been tense for Cee-Cee for quite a while. She had been looking at a lot of time behind bars and now, suddenly, she had been given her life back. The deputy's voice finally boomed into Cee's room over the speaker: "Roll it up." We all turned to take one last look at our outspoken friend. She went to her cell, gathered up her bedroll and personal belongings, came out, kicked her door shut and dropped her things to the floor. Hugging Kori tightly, she told her to stay strong and that if Kori didn't write, she would tell LaTesha to sit on her. "I'll do it, too, lil' white girl," LaTesha threatened. "Ain't nothin' funny about it." Cee-Cee then came over and gave me a friendly hug and a hearty slap on the back. She stuck a crumpled piece of paper in my hand and said, "The same goes for you as Kori. If I don't hear from you, you're in big trouble." She winked at me, picked up her stuff and headed out the door.

I opened my hand to examine the wad of paper inside. I unfolded it and read the following:

To Jen,

Thanks for being my freind [sic]. I like your persenality [sic] and like you a lot. I hope we can be freinds [sic] for ever. Don't forget me and please write.

Cee-Cee

I gently folded the paper and placed it in my pocket. Although we corresponded for a time after her release, Cee-Cee's letters eventually tapered off and ended, and I knew she was back in the streets, immersed in her favorite vices again. After my own release, I never saw or heard from Cee-Cee again.

The day after Cee-Cee departed OCWJ, I sat down in my usual spot in the dayroom and began reading the newspaper as I did every morning. There, tucked away insignificantly on one of the back pages, was an article about the passing of a quiet, older inmate I had known named Rose. Rose was in for drug (heroin) and prostitution charges. She was a very poor, but dignified, 54-year-old Hispanic woman who had come to the United States in her teens as an illegal immigrant seeking a better life, but had spent the intervening years being taken advantage of and abused in every form imaginable on the streets. Rose was self-contained aloof and never participated in the pettiness that went on among the other women. When she spoke, she spoke about one thing: her son, David. He was twenty-years-old and in the Navy and living a very respectable life. There was no light behind her eyes unless she was speaking of her boy or looking at his photo. When the news came, it was very apparent that even the deputies who had to relay it were crushed. David had been killed in a single-vehicle accident. He had driven off the highway late at night on his way back to the base and the car rolled several times. Rose was devastated. She was permitted to go to her son's funeral, and the remainder of her sentence was waived. She was free. A week after David's funeral, Rose stepped off a curb into the path of a city bus. When I read the article, I knew it wasn't an accident. She used to say that she had done everything in her life wrong, except for her son. He was the only thing she had done right, and he was everything in the world to her. He had literally been her only hope and without him, there was nothing good left in the world for her. Such a beautiful name, Rose, for such a tragic life.

These tragedies continue and grow and are passed down through generations of people living on the streets of Orange County, one of the most "all-American," wealthiest and most conservative areas of the country. The struggles and obstacles that these individuals face from birth are overlooked and minimized when society dismisses them as low-lifes unworthy of compassion, understanding or assistance. When I left OCWJ, Whitney Millano was on her 17th visit for drug and prostitution charges. The woman whose mother sold her for drugs when she was 2, and whose father then decapitated her mother. This woman who grew up in an orphanage and in extremely abusive foster homes. Our taxpayer dollars are going toward confining her in a small space for months at a time, seventeen times, with no attempts to help her learn to actually function in a normal manner when she's on the outside. This is an absurd waste of money and a tragic lack of civilized compassion that is repeated thousands of times a day in our criminal justice system. These are not evil miscreants who were born to alternately terrorize society and live in confined misery. These are human beings who have suffered tremendously and whose criminal acts derive directly from that suffering. By focusing on revenge and punishment rather than understanding and rehabilitation, we not only increase the suffering, but also the number of future victims. It is a short-sighted and emotion-based response to criminal behavior, and until we begin taking a more rational approach, the Roses, Cee-Cees and Whitneys of the world will continue to multiply. If it's happening in the idyllic and perfectly-preened "O.C.," one can only imagine the degree to which it is occurring in less financially-blessed communities. If we are truly a civilized and humane country, rehabilitation must take precedence over retribution, and we must address the insidious and painful sources of criminal behavior.

Although there were moments of levity at OCWJ, there were many more moments that felt like the dark ages: Twenty-two hours a day restricted to a 6' x 8' cell; deprived of all contact with family, friends and pets; being woken in the middle of the night to have your person and cell searched; being ordered to strip or do anything a deputy requests at any moment; sleeping on a cold, hard mat in a concrete room, etc. It would pain most people to force their pet dog or cat to endure such conditions over months or years, but we often gleefully inflict such punishment upon our fellow humans. Jail was the first place I experienced night terrors, and I've never forgotten the profoundly intense feelings of horror, grief and loss. The intensity of the terror is literally beyond description. It still haunts me today, in spite of all my attempts to get past it and move on. Until we begin treating each other as humanely as we treat our pets, and until we recognize the value of rehabilitation over retribution, we can never truly call ourselves civilized, and we will continue to contribute to the suffering in the world.

ORANGE COUNTY WOMEN'S JAIL

You can chain me, you can torture me, you can even destroy this body, but you will never imprison my mind.

~Mahatma Gandhi

EPILOGUE

Following my trial and my eventual release from OCWJ, I returned to school, obtained my Master's Degree in Psychology and embarked on a career as a researcher and writer. I remained in touch with a few of the women I met while incarcerated, but over time our connections were lost. On the pages that follow are reprints of newspaper articles that reference what became of some of the individuals mentioned in this book:

ORANGE COUNTY WOMEN'S JAIL

Ardith Cribbs

Orange County Register (California)

March 30, 1996 Saturday MORNING EDITION

Woman who murdered mate gets 30 years to life; COURTS: Prosecutor said financial gain and a buildup of emotions were motives for the slaying.

BYLINE: BRYON MacWILLIAMS, The Orange County Register
SECTION: METRO; Pg. B04

A woman who fatally shot her husband and then lost her bid to be found not guilty by reason of insanity was sentenced Friday to 30 years to life in state prison.

The maximum term was imposed against Ardith M. Cribbs, 39, who fired five bullets into the legs, groin, back and skull of Gordon L. Cribbs in 1994 while he was nude and handcuffed to a bedpost in their house in Huntington Beach.

She was unflinching as the family of her husband, a high-ranking official with the state Department of Fish and Game, addressed Superior Court Judge Francisco P. Briseno.

"I know that he loved Ardith, and was willing to do whatever he could to give her a life, and love her," an older brother, Harold Cribbs, said during the proceeding in Santa Ana. "We accepted her as part of our family," he said. "But she never loved him and set about to kill him long before she committed the act. We found that she was a cold, calculating, unprincipled individual."

"Some people come into this world and give. He was one of those," added another older brother, Daniel. "Others pass through and leave no mark. And some take. This woman took."

Gordon Cribbs' daughter, Kendra, sobbed uncontrollably after she made eye contact with her father's killer. She told Briseno she is only able to sleep with a light on and fears leaving the doors and windows unlocked. "She was just so evil," said Kendra Cribbs. "I feel that she degraded my father the way that she killed him, and went about it. "

And the victim's son, Sean Cribbs, said, "My father was a stand-up guy who always did right by others. He was made of all the stuff that is good in the world."

Briseno, who appeared to hold back tears, thanked the victim's family for sharing their feelings. He termed the killing "brutal" and "completely unwarranted."

Ardith Cribbs' attorney, Peter Larkin, asked for a base term of 28 years in light of his client's turbulent history; she attempted suicide numerous times, suffered from sleeping and eating disorders and believed someone was monitoring her through a device implanted in her brain.

"This isn't something that was made up. Her mental instability goes back many years," said Larkin, who stressed earlier that she had been sexually molested between ages 6 and 16.

But Deputy District Attorney Carolyn Kirkwood had argued to jurors that the defendant was in control of most aspects of her life. Financial gain, as well as a buildup of angry emotions, were motives for the Aug. 10 slaying, she said.

Court testimony showed Ardith Cribbs worked as a prostitute at two Nevada brothels before meeting Gordon, her fourth husband, in Long Beach.

JENNIFER SWEET

Lisa Peng

The Associated Press State & Local Wire

October 12, 2001, Friday, BC cycle

Parents of slain Chinese woman sue killer, husband

SECTION: State and Regional
DATELINE: SANTA ANA, Calif.

The parents of a Chinese woman killed by her millionaire lover's jealous wife have filed a wrongful-death lawsuit against the couple.

Li-Yun "Lisa" Peng pleaded guilty in June to voluntary manslaughter in the 1993 slaying of Ranbing "Jennifer" Ji, 25, and the mistress' 5-month-old son, Kevin, in their Mission Viejo apartment.

The guilty plea followed three unsuccessful prosecutions - two ending in hung juries and the third in a conviction that was tossed out on appeal.

As part of the plea Peng was deported to Taiwan.

The lawsuit, filed in Orange County Superior Court, does not specify the amount of damages sought. A federal court recently rejected a similar claim filed on behalf of Ji and her son.

The complaint alleges that Jim Peng was responsible for the killings because he had an affair with Ji that became public knowledge, driving his wife to a murderous rage.

The case with its elements of wealth, lust and revenge was followed closely by residents of China, Taiwan and other Asian countries. A movie about the case was filmed in Taiwan.

Electronics tycoon Tseng "Jim" Peng's worth was estimated at $200 million, most of it from his Ranger Communications which made CB radios in Asia.

JENNIFER SWEET

Cynthia Medina

Orange County Register (California)

January 26, 1997 Sunday MORNING EDITION

METRO UPDATE;
THE FOLLOW-UP FILE

BYLINE: KEN NIEDZIELA;RON GONZALES, The Orange County Register
SECTION: METRO; Pg. B03

Mom's conviction for torturing boys upheld on appeal.

THEN: Cynthia Medina in May 1995 became the first person in Orange County to be convicted of torture. Medina, of Orange, was sentenced to life in prison for sexually torturing her 10-year-old nephew and physically abusing her 9-year-old son. She burned the nephew's tongue with a hot butter knife, whipped him with an electrical cord and sodomized him twice with a small wooden baseball bat, prosecutors said.

The episode on Sept. 7, 1994, occurred because the boy lied after he was seen touching an ashtray in which Medina had left the remains of a marijuana cigarette. Her husband, Edward Medina, was sentenced to two years in prison for failing to stop or report the abuse.

NOW: The 4th District Court of Appeal on Jan. 17 refused to overturn Cynthia Medina's conviction. Medina appealed on several grounds, among them claims that the evidence was insufficient and her sentence was cruel and unusual punishment. The court also denied her argument that the torture statute is unconstitutionally vague. She cited the statute's use of the phrases "cruel pain," "any sadistic purpose" and "torture."

Writing for the court, Justice Edward Wallin said, "One who repeatedly burns the tongue of a minor victim and sticks even a small baseball bat up his rectum to extract a confession cannot be heard to complain, 'How was I to know that might be considered torture?'" The court said her sentence wasn't excessive. "The conduct in this case constituted classic torture for a classic reason, to force the victim to talk," Wallin wrote. "In this case, the punishment fits the crime. "

JENNIFER SWEET

Edward Patrick Morgan

Los Angeles Times

November 27, 2010 Saturday
Home Edition

Inmates on death row wait years for lawyers; The backlog is blamed on sparse state funds, the emotional toll and long odds of success.

BYLINE: Maura Dolan
SECTION: LATEXTRA; Metro Desk; Part AA; Pg. 1

Thirteen years ago, Edward Patrick Morgan asked the California Supreme Court for a lawyer to investigate and challenge his 1996 death sentence for a murder in Orange County. The court has yet to find Morgan an attorney.

The inability of the state to recruit lawyers for post-conviction challenges, or habeas corpus petitions, has caused a major bottleneck in the state's criminal justice system. Nearly half of those condemned to die in California are awaiting appointment of counsel for these challenges.

This "critical shortage," as the state high court describes it, has persisted for years, despite lawyer gluts. The average wait for these attorneys is 10 to 12 years.

Criminal defense lawyers attribute the scarcity to inadequate state funding, the emotional toll of representing a client facing execution and the likelihood that the California Supreme Court will uphold a capital conviction.

Earlier this year, the California Supreme Court accepted a cursory post-conviction challenge from Morgan. The court permitted Morgan's petition to be a mere place-holder until an attorney could be found to file a proper one.

By accepting it, the court spared Morgan from missing a key legal deadline while still giving him the opportunity to challenge his sentence later on.

Atty. Gen. Jerry Brown had urged the court to reject Morgan's "shell petition," arguing that the court's practice of permitting them has delayed the resolution of capital cases.

But Justice Joyce L. Kennard, writing for the court, said it would be "grossly unfair" to require "an indigent death row inmate who is untrained in the law" to prepare his own post-conviction challenge.

"What is causing the delay...," Kennard wrote, "is not that practice but this court's inability so far to recruit qualified habeas corpus counsel for each of the hundreds of death row inmates."

JENNIFER SWEET

Los Angeles Times

July 20, 1996, Saturday, Orange County Edition

JUDGE SENTENCES MORGAN TO DEATH; COURTS: RAPIST WAS CONVICTED OF 1994 MURDER OF LEANORA ANNETTE WONG OUTSIDE A NIGHTCLUB. HER FAMILY VOWS TO WITNESS EXECUTION.

BYLINE: ANNA CEKOLA, TIMES STAFF WRITER
SECTION: Metro; Part B; Page 1; Metro Desk
DATELINE: SANTA ANA

A rapist did not say a word Friday as a judge sentenced him to die for strangling and sexually mutilating a young woman he had just met at an Orange nightclub.

Superior Court Judge Richard L. Weatherspoon cited "overwhelming" evidence in upholding a jury's decision that 30-year-old Edward Patrick Morgan should be executed.

Morgan declined to make a statement on his behalf, while the parents of his victim, 23-year-old Leanora Annette Wong, left court in tears. They vowed to witness Morgan's death.

"I'm just glad it's all over," said Nora Wong, her eyes red from crying. "Of course, it can't bring back our daughter."

Morgan was convicted of the May 20, 1994, kidnapping, sexual assault and murder of Wong, a UC Riverside graduate who had recently moved to Orange County to help manage a footwear store.

During his trial, Morgan apologized for killing Wong in what he contended was a drunken rage. He said he didn't care if he lived or died.

"There's nothing worse than doing something you can't undo," he told the jury.

Wong's family said the remorse is meaningless.

"He should have thought about it before he killed somebody," Nora Wong said. "Now he says sorry. That doesn't help."

Family members sent a letter to the court describing their pain and sleepless nights since Leanora's death.

"A lot of times I wish that night will not come and also I cannot eat and have lost weight," Nora Wong wrote. "It took my husband over three months before he went back to work and our son has lost his only sister and he was very angry."

Morgan had been paroled from prison just weeks before he met Wong at the now-defunct Australian Beach Club. He invited her to walk outside, then forced her into a secluded enclosure, where he beat and strangled her, according to testimony.

Wong's body, battered and mutilated with a sharp object, was found the next morning.

Part of the attack was captured on a surveillance camera. Investigators found Morgan's bloody handprint at the scene.

Morgan has a history of crimes against women that includes three previous convictions for sexual assault that landed him in state prison.

The defendant's attorney conceded his client inflicted "unspeakable" wounds on Wong, but said Morgan acted in a "blind rage" and didn't plan on killing her.

The defense called no witnesses on his behalf until the trial's penalty phase, when former teachers described him as a hard-working athlete and friends recalled his explosive temper. Jurors were shown school records indicating Morgan was an "emotionally disturbed" child who had a poor relationship with his parents, especially his mother. Morgan, who maintains a body-builder's physique, was placed in special-education classes throughout his schooling in La Palma.

Defense attorney Julian Bailey said the death sentence only "compounds the tragedy" and will generate years of costly appeals.

Taxpayer dollars, Bailey said, would be better-spent helping children with problems like Morgan had.

"He was difficult to deal with. But if you deal with the difficult kids, maybe you won't have to deal with horrible criminal behavior like this when they become adults," Bailey said.

Deputy Dist. Atty. Lewis Rosenblum had said Morgan deserved to die for using his looks and charm to entice Wong to an especially brutal death.

"This is the most horrific crime that I've ever seen in my career in law enforcement," Orange Police Det. Patrick Thayer said Friday.

"There's no forgiving for something like this."

JENNIFER SWEET

Antoinette Yancey

Orange County Register (California)

March 3, 2011 Thursday

Death row: Robbery leads to murder at F.V. store

BYLINE: By LARRY WELBORN, THE ORANGE COUNTY REGISTER
SECTION: FOUNTAINVALLEY; Pg. B

The Orange County Register is publishing summaries of the 58 killers sentenced to death by Orange County judges, two per day during weekdays, from the oldest case to the newest.
No. 27 – 1997:

William Clinton Clark was convicted of masterminding a 1991 computer-store robbery where Kathy Lee, the mother of an employee, was slain when she arrived at the Fountain Valley store to pick up her son, an employee. Clark also was convicted of convincing his girlfriend to murder a witness to the first crime. Ardell Love Williams, 19, was lured to a location with a promise of a job in 1994 and shot to death before she could testify against Clark. Clark's girlfriend, Antoinette Yancey, was sentenced to life without parole for her role in the Williams' slaying.
-- Researcher Michael Doss contributed to this report

ORANGE COUNTY WOMEN'S JAIL

Los Angeles Times

December 30, 1997, Tuesday, Orange County Edition

DEATH PENALTY FOR MASTERMIND; COURTS: JUDGE CONDEMNS WILLIAM CLINTON CLARK FOR KILLINGS EVEN THOUGH HE DIDN'T PULL THE TRIGGER.

BYLINE: GREG HERNANDEZ, TIMES STAFF WRITER
SECTION: Metro; Part B; Page 1; Metro Desk
DATELINE: SANTA ANA

Becoming the first person to be condemned in Orange County for two murders at which he was not present, William Clinton Clark was sentenced Monday to die for masterminding a botched robbery that resulted in one death, then ordering the execution of a witness in the case.

Judge John J. Ryan said that even though Clark did not commit either murder, he was responsible for both.

"I think the evidence in this case, while largely circumstantial, was absolutely overwhelming," Ryan said.

Before imposing the death sentence, Ryan allowed the defendant to speak for more than an hour, then took the unusual step of responding directly to his remarks.

Clark, 44, of Los Angeles, insisted that he had "never hurt anybody" and lashed out at the prosecutor, police and witnesses in the case, all of whom he said lied to obtain a conviction.

"You don't care," Clark said at one point, looking prosecutor Rick King in the eye. "You want me to die."

Clark, who is African American, also said that race played a part in his conviction on murder charges that he maintains were not proved in court.

"Let's execute the black man," Clark said. "No one cares. I'm a black man. You can do anything you want to do with me."

The defendant said his trial was "total fantasy and so far removed from reality."

At one point, King requested that Clark be sworn in so the prosecutor could challenge the defendant's comments in a cross-examination. But the judge denied the request and let Clark complete his statement uninterrupted.

Ryan then responded, pointing out that, during Clark's stinging remarks, the defendant failed to mention any of the incriminating evidence against him.

"Your fantasies about this case may well sell books, but I didn't find them very convincing," Ryan said.

In October, a jury found Clark guilty of planning the 1991 robbery of a Fountain Valley computer store. Kathy Lee, 49, was shot in the head during the holdup. He also was convicted of arranging the execution-style murder of Ardell Love Williams, 22, in 1994 after she agreed to testify against him.

Ryan acknowledged Monday that Clark was "disappointed" and "surprised" by Lee's murder.

"That's the problem with a takeover robbery," Ryan said. "It's foreseeable that somebody's going to get hurt."

Of victim Williams, who had been a friend of Clark's, the judge said, "She violated Mr. Clark's code: Don't snitch. And for that reason, she was murdered."

Williams' mother sobbed and slumped in her seat as an emotional video highlighting her daughter's life played to a silent courtroom. She also shook her head in disgust a few times during Clark's lengthy remarks.

Angie Williams, 61, has suffered through the murders of two of her nine daughters. In 1985, Tina Williams was found bludgeoned to death in Culver City in a crime that was never solved.

"They say time goes by and it's easier," Angie Williams said Monday. "But no, it's not."

The victim's older sister, Fay Williams Scott, said it was Tina Williams' unsolved murder that led Ardell Williams to agree to testify against Clark. Scott said her sister wanted to help ease the grief of Kathy Lee's family.

Lee, a secretary from Garden Grove, was killed when she arrived to pick up her teenage son from a CompUSA store in Fountain Valley. She arrived just as the robbery was taking place.

Lee's husband, Peter, said the death penalty for Clark "is certainly justified."

"He's not a nice person," said Lee, who had been married to his wife for 27 years. "I'm just thankful that six years of murder trials are finally over."

He said his son, also named Peter, has taken his mother's murder hard.

"He doesn't come around very much," the father said. "I guess he probably feels responsible for her death."

Ardell Williams did not actually witness the shooting but had been with Clark about a month before the robbery when he cased the computer store. She learned about Lee's murder from Clark's younger brother and told authorities what she knew.

The triggerman in the computer store robbery and Clark's younger brother both are serving life sentences without parole for Lee's murder. Clark's girlfriend, Antoinette Yancey, was convicted of murder last year and sentenced to life without parole for her role in the Williams slaying.

In May 1996, Clark was convicted of double first-degree murder. But the jury was unable to decide whether he should be executed, and the question was posed to a second jury this fall.

Clark's trials were the first in recent Orange County history involving someone charged with killing a witness. King said the killing of a witness has "a significant impact on the system."

"He made the decision to basically assassinate the witness that came forward who implicated him in the first murder," King said. "He's going to forfeit his life for those acts."

Outside court, defense attorney Rob Harley said he challenged the credibility of witnesses in the case who he believed "were pushing the limits."

"I am greatly saddened," Harley said of the death sentence. "I felt we had a decent shot at getting a life sentence. He wasn't the triggerman, and we obviously disagree with the judge's decision. But we can't do anything about it."

Even though he had argued before two juries that Clark should be executed, King said he took no joy in the outcome of the case.

"It's not a happy day," the prosecutor said. "But it was a just thing. We were very thankful the judge in this case saw the evidence the same way the jury did."

ORANGE COUNTY WOMEN'S JAIL

John Famalaro

Orange County Register (California)

July 9, 2011 Saturday

Death affirmed for woman's killer

BYLINE: LARRY WELBORN REGISTER WRITER, The Orange County Register
SECTION: LOCAL; Pg. B

HIGHLIGHT: Court holds that John Famalaro received fair trial in Denise Huber's kidnapping, assault and murder.

The California Supreme Court has affirmed the death penalty given to a Laguna Hills man who was convicted of kidnapping, sexually assaulting and murdering a 23-year-old Newport Beach woman in 1991, then keeping her handcuffed body in a freezer for three years as a trophy.

In a unanimous decision published on Thursday, the Supreme Court found that John Famalaro, now 60, received a fair trial in Orange County in 1997 for the murder of Denise Huber, who was abducted when her car broke down on the 73 late at night on June 23, 1991.

Orange County Deputy District Attorney Christopher Evans argued during Famalaro's trial in 1997 that Famalaro took Huber to a warehouse in

Laguna Hills, where he sexually assaulted her and bludgeoned her to death.

Famalaro then stored the nude, battered and handcuffed body in a freezer he bought a few days after the slaying, and kept it for three years while Huber's parents and friends frantically searched for her.

His scheme was uncovered in July 1994 when sheriff's deputies in Yavapai County, Arizona, investigated a report of a stolen rental truck, and came across the freezer in the back of the truck, powered by an extension cord from the small house where Famalaro was living.

Deputies cut through a padlock on the freezer and three layers of plastic trash bags before they found Huber's naked body, frozen solid in a fetal position with the hands secured behind the back with metal handcuffs.

Famalaro's arrest and subsequent trial drew intense media attention as he was extradited from Arizona and tried in Orange County.

His trial was covered by newspapers, radio station and television stations. It became a true-crime book, "Cold Storage," written by Garden Grove author Dan Lasseter.

And it was listed by The Orange County Register in 2009 as one of the most notorious cases in county history.

Famalaro's appellate court attorneys claimed that he was denied a fair trial in part because of that media attention.

They argued that his trial should have been moved out of Orange County because of prejudicial pre-trial publicity that allegedly contaminated the jury pool.

But the Supreme Court, in a 56-page decision authored by Justice Joyce Kennard, disagreed. They found that Orange County Superior Court Judge John J. Ryan properly conducted the jury selection process and qualified a jury that was fair and unbiased.

"True, the jury selection process indicated that defendant's case was well known in Orange County, and that there was considerable community sentiment that he was guilty of murdering Denise and should be executed for that crime," Kennard wrote.

"Here, our independent review ... shows that the selection process resulted in a panel of jurors untainted by the publicity surrounding this case, and we see no evidence that any of them held biases that the selection process failed to detect."

The decision to affirm Famalaro's death sentence does not mean that his potential execution is imminent in California, where there is an informal moratorium on capital punishment while lawyers battle the legality of lethal injection as a means of execution.

His defense team will also take their appeals to the Supreme Court, a process that could take years to resolve.

Famalaro will remain on death row at San Quentin State Prison, one of 58 killers from Orange County sentenced to death.

ORANGE COUNTY WOMEN'S JAIL

Maria Martinez

Los Angeles Times

August 4, 1995, Friday, Orange County Edition

KIDNAPER OF INFANT GETS 8-YEAR SENTENCE; CRIME: ON EVE OF TRIAL, MARIA LUISA MARTINEZ OF DELANO PLEADS GUILTY TO TAKING THE 4-MONTH-OLD SANTA ANA GIRL FROM A SOUTH COAST PLAZA STORE IN APRIL.

BYLINE: By KEN ELLINGWOOD, TIMES STAFF WRITER
SECTION: Metro; Part B; Page 4; Metro Desk
DATELINE: SANTA ANA

A Central Valley woman was sentenced to eight years in prison Thursday after admitting she snatched a Santa Ana infant from a shopping mall in April.

On the eve of her trial on kidnapping charges, Maria Luisa Martinez, 37, of Delano, pleaded guilty to face up to her deed, her lawyer said.

"She wanted to accept responsibility for what she had done. It was bothering her conscience," said Deputy Public Defender Marion Wheeler. "She felt bad about how the parents felt."

Superior Court Judge Anthony Rackauckas cited Martinez's lack of a criminal record in sparing her the maximum sentence of 11 years and 8 months.

The parents of Steffany Zamora, who was 4 months old at the time of the April 22 kidnapping, avoided the sentencing because they did not want to be near Martinez, said a lawyer representing them.

But in a written statement read in court by the lawyer, Mario and Beatriz Zamora said they were glad Martinez was being sent to prison.

"This is a very happy day for Mr. and Mrs. Zamora," lawyer Christine K. Roberts said. Attempts to reach the Zamoras for comments were unsuccessful.

In April, Martinez, who had met the family a short time earlier, and Steffany's aunt took the infant to have her picture taken at a Sear's department store at South Coast Plaza. Martinez disappeared with the girl when the aunt went to make a telephone call. The family hunted desperately, distributing flyers and getting widespread media attention. An anonymous tip led police to Martinez a week later, and the child was found unharmed.

Wheeler said he did not know Martinez's motive for kidnapping the girl. He said defense investigators could not confirm Martinez's claim that her own baby had died in childbirth in Mexico last fall -- eliminating a possible defense that she was suffering post-birth depression.

"Her situation is almost pathetic," Wheeler said. "She's probably one of the saddest situations I've seen."

He that is taken and put into prison or chains is not conquered, though overcome; for he is still an enemy.

~Thomas Hobbes

It isn't true that convicts live like animals:

animals have more room to move around.

~Mario Vargas Llosa

ORANGE COUNTY WOMEN'S JAIL

To assert in any case that a man must be absolutely cut off from society because he is absolutely evil amounts to saying that society is absolutely good, and no-one in his right mind will believe this today.

~Albert Camus

JENNIFER SWEET

Two men look out the same prison bars;

One sees mud and the other stars.

~Beck

ORANGE COUNTY WOMEN'S JAIL

It costs $30,000 to $50,000 per year to send someone to jail. You don't have to pay so much to send someone to school at Johns Hopkins.

~John Money

I know not whether Laws be right or

whether Laws be wrong; all that we know

who live in jail is that the wall is strong;

and that each day is like a year;

a year whose days are long.

~Oscar Wilde

ORANGE COUNTY WOMEN'S JAIL

One of the many lessons that one learns in prison is that things are what they are, and will be what they will be.

~Oscar Wilde

What I learned in jail is that I can't change.

I can't live a different lifestyle — this is it.

This is the life that they gave,

and this is the life that I made.

~Tupac Shakur

ORANGE COUNTY WOMEN'S JAIL

I don't like jail. They've got the wrong kind of bars in there.

~Charles Bukowski

In prison, those things withheld from and denied to the prisoner become precisely what he wants most of all.

~Eldridge Cleaver

ORANGE COUNTY WOMEN'S JAIL

I submit that an individual who breaks the law that conscience tells him is unjust and willingly accepts the penalty by staying in jail to arouse the conscience of the community over its injustice, is in reality expressing the very highest respect for the law.

~Martin Luther King, Jr.

So what really works? Treatments in jail do some good, but it's mostly too late: finding a family and a job or just growing older make most prisoners eventually give up crime.

~Polly Toynbee

ORANGE COUNTY WOMEN'S JAIL

We who live in prison, and in whose lives

there is no event but sorrow,

have to measure time by throbs of pain,

and the record of bitter moments.

~Oscar Wilde

I know what it's like to be ignored, and I think that is the big problem about the prison system: These people are being thrown away. There is no sense of rehabilitation. In some places, they are trying to do things. But, in most cases, it's a holding cell.

~Lee Tergesen

ORANGE COUNTY WOMEN'S JAIL

Such is the remorseless progression of human society, shedding lives and souls as it goes on its way. It is an ocean into which men sink who have been cast out by the law and consigned, with help most cruelly withheld, to moral death. The sea is the pitiless social darkness into which the penal system casts those it has condemned, an unfathomable waste of misery. The human soul, lost in those depths, may become a corpse.
Who shall revive it?

~Victor Hugo

T 34034

H.S. LMC Brillion, WI

DATE DUE

MAY 07 2012			
MAY 21 2012			

Demco, Inc. 38-293

12814540R00087

Made in the USA
Lexington, KY
03 January 2012